Rejuvenating Introductory Courses

Associate Dean, Teaching & Research

Karen I. Spear, *Editor*

NEW DIRECTIONS FOR TEACHING AND LEARNING

KENNETH E. EBLE, *Editor-in-Chief*

Number 20, December 1984

Paperback sourcebooks in
The Jossey-Bass Higher Education Series

Jossey-Bass Inc., Publishers
San Francisco • Washington • London

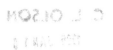

Karen I. Spear (Ed.).
Rejuvenating Introductory Courses.
New Directions for Teaching and Learning, no. 20.
San Francisco: Jossey-Bass, 1984.

New Directions for Teaching and Learning Series
Kenneth E. Eble, *Editor-in-Chief*

New Directions for Teaching and Learning is published quarterly
by Jossey-Bass Inc., Publishers. Subscriptions, single-issue
orders, change of address notices, undelivered copies, and other
correspondence should be sent to Subscriptions, Jossey-Bass Inc.,
Publishers, 433 California Street, San Francisco, California 94104.

Editorial correspondence should be sent to the Editor-in-Chief,
Kenneth E. Eble, Department of English, University of Utah,
Salt Lake City, Utah 84112.

Library of Congress Catalogue Card Number LC 83-82086
International Standard Serial Number ISSN 0271-0633
International Standard Book Number ISBN 87589-793-2

Cover art by Willi Baum
Manufactured in the United States of America

Ordering Information

The paperback sourcebooks listed below are published quarterly and can be ordered either by subscription or single-copy.
Subscriptions cost $35.00 per year for institutions, agencies, and libraries. Individuals can subscribe at the special rate of $25.00 per year *if payment is by personal check.* (Note that the full rate of $35.00 applies if payment is by institutional check, even if the subscription is designated for an individual.) Standing orders are accepted. Subscriptions normally begin with the first of the four sourcebooks in the current publication year of the series. When ordering, please indicate if you prefer your subscription to begin with the first issue of the *coming* year.
Single copies are available at $8.95 when payment accompanies order, and *all single-copy orders under $25.00 must include payment.* (California, New Jersey, New York, and Washington, D.C., residents please include appropriate sales tax.) For billed orders, cost per copy is $8.95 plus postage and handling. (Prices subject to change without notice.)
Bulk orders (ten or more copies) of any individual sourcebook are available at the following discounted prices: 10–49 copies, $8.05 each; 50–100 copies, $7.15 each; over 100 copies, *inquire.* Sales tax and postage and handling charges apply as for single copy orders.
To ensure correct and prompt delivery, all orders must give either the *name of an individual* or an *official purchase order number.* Please submit your order as follows:

Subscriptions: specify series and year subscription is to begin.
Single Copies: specify sourcebook code (such as, TL8) and first two words of title.

Mail orders for United States and Possessions, Latin America, Canada, Japan, Australia, and New Zealand to:
Jossey-Bass Inc., Publishers
433 California Street
San Francisco, California 94104

Mail orders for all other parts of the world to:
Jossey-Bass Limited
28 Banner Street
London EC1Y 8QE

New Directions for Teaching and Learning Series
Kenneth E. Eble, *Editor-in-Chief*

Contents

Editor's Notes

Introductory courses are as much a fixture of academic life as chalk-boards. They affect every student at every institution of higher learning. Introductory courses mark the beginning of a student's exposure to a discipline, providing the foundation for subsequent study. For students who enroll in introductory courses to meet their liberal education requirements, introductory courses also mark endings. They make up the totality of a student's acquaintance with a discipline that is otherwise unrelated to the student's major. For all students, introductory courses stand as the gateway to higher education, creating indelible impressions about majors, careers, and personal, social, and intellectual values. For the significant number of students who leave college either by design or by default after their sophomore year to become workers, voters, taxpayers, and parents, introductory courses represent what college is all about.

Despite the importance of introductory courses both to the student population and to the long-term health of higher education, few features of teaching and learning have been more neglected. No books and very few articles have been written on introductory courses. What discussion there is appears within larger considerations of general education or the internal planning of specific institutions. Except for the rapid expansion of knowledge into new disciplines and new academic departments—each of which develops its own introductory course—the introductory courses, like classroom chalkboards, remain essentially the same from one institution to another, from one generation to another. The introductory course conjures up images that are all too familiar: a sea of faces in a lecture hall, each one looking earnest, determined, and resigned to be educated; oversize textbooks stuffed under straight-backed chairs bolted to the floor; hands scribbling madly to transcribe information delivered by a lecturer from dogeared yellow lecture notes—or by a nervous teaching assistant trying desperately to keep the class from drifting into areas she has not yet studied herself.

Introductory courses suffer from benign neglect. Comfortably maintained by tradition, they are bolstered by the needs of college and department, major and nonmajor alike. Thus, they are taught primarily for convenience so both faculty and students can get on with more interesting work in intermediate, upper-division, or graduate courses. This sourcebook offers a critical examination of introductory courses:

1

what they are and are not, what they should do for beginning students, and how they might be most effectively taught. The criticisms of introductory courses raised here fall into two broad areas — conceptual shortcomings and pedagogical shortcomings. Conceptual shortcomings involve questions of audience and purpose. With these questions unanswered, introductory courses suffer from an array of pedagogical ills.

Conceptual Shortcomings

Who Are Introductory Courses for? Introductory courses attract a diverse audience with quite varied needs: students beginning work in their major, some of whom think they intend to go on to graduate school; others, like teaching majors, who need the course to serve their vocational needs; liberal education students; students with undeclared majors; and students who are simply looking for an interesting way to fill elective hours. Both pedagogy and rhetoric require that courses should be suited to their audience. But, with enrollments as varied as these, introductory courses risk being everything to everyone and easily become nothing to anyone. For instance, the needs of majors and nonmajors may be so different that teaching to one set of students is to neglect the other. Sensitive to these different needs, the Carnegie Foundation recommends that departments should develop introductory courses specifically for nonmajors that avoid the intellectual shallowness of appreciation courses and convey "the history, concerns, and method of inquiry in [the given] field" (Carnegie Foundation for the Advancement of Teaching, 1977, p. 170). In Chapter Five, Elof Carlson reports on the development of a course in the life sciences for nonmajors and describes how courses in biology for majors and nonmajors differ. His chapter speaks to the larger question of how the needs of majors and nonmajors diverge across the curriculum.

What Are the Goals of Introductory Courses? Many chapters in this volume ask questions about the most fruitful approach to the introductory course. Their authors suspect that the most successful introductions for students of all kinds are those that place the larger questions, concepts, and methods of field in the context of genuine human problems. In Chapter Six, David Winter is critical of introductions to psychology (and, by extension, of introductions to the other social sciences) that have become narrowly defined introductions to the undergraduate major program, the first steps toward an advanced degree and a career in the discipline. Such courses exercise students' ability to remember vocabulary, definitions of terms, theories, and other pieces of information as they rush through crowded units that represent key topics in the discipline.

Gamson and Associates (1984) offer one reason for this state of affairs. Reviewing undergraduate education since World War II, these authors point to the substantial increase in federal support for research, the dramatic expansion of graduate education after Sputnik, and the increase in faculty control within institutions during the early 1960s. These factors led faculty to stop thinking of themselves as educators and to start seeing themselves as biologists, historians, sociologists, and so forth. The result, as Harriet W. Sheridan shows in Chapter One, is a faculty unwilling or perhaps unable to examine fundamental assumptions in their discipline or to devote much energy to arousing interest among the uninitiated. Booth's address to the Modern Language Association (1983, p. 319), states the problem succinctly: "Give us lovers, and we will love them, but do not expect us to study courtship."

The contributors to this volume suggest that introductory courses have strayed in the wrong direction for majors and nonmajors alike. Instead of being dominated by a concern for the vocabulary and taxonomy that are presumed necessary for further study in the discipline, introductory courses should be organized around the liberal education ideals of critical analysis, problem solving, the formation and expression of values associated with the discipline, and the development of an understanding of the nature and process of inquiry as it is conducted from one field to another. In Chapter Seven, William Whisner draws on the work of John Dewey to argue that the introductory philosophy course must psychologize the subject, beginning with the philosophical questions that are already of concern to students, in order to engage them in the process of examining and formulating their beliefs rationally. In Chapter Two, Marshall W. Gregory takes a more general perspective. He argues that introductory courses are introductions not just to a discipline but to the cultivation of mind that is the fundamental goal of education.

The work of cognitive psychologists David Ausubel (1975) and Jerome Bruner (1973) lends empirical support to arguments for the necessity of developing courses around significant issues. Their studies of learning and cognition suggest that reserving study of significant problems for upper-division or graduate study while trying to pile up facts in the beginning course puts the cart before the horse. Without an understanding of the larger questions and problems of a field, students can do no more than commit to short-term memory the unassimilated data that are part of the field. Ausubel (1975, p. 96) insists that learning requires a framework of "those unifying concepts and propositions in a given discipline that have the widest explanatory power, inclusiveness, generalizability, and relatability to the subject matter of that discipline." He describes the organization of thought as hierarchical, with the most inclusive ideas allowing one to comprehend "progressively less inclusive and more highly differentiated propositions, concepts, and factual data" (p. 100). His criticisms of teaching parallel those of the contributors to this sourcebook: Introductory courses are usually arranged serially, not hierarchically, and they place more emphasis on details of the new topic than on the ideas and theories that organize it.

Like Ausubel, Bruner (1973) finds this approach at odds both with the nature of learning and with the character of any discipline. In his essay "The Perfectibility of Intellect," Bruner (1973, p. 17) observes that "man creates theories before he creates tools," emphasizing that the theory, hunch, question, or need must precede the creation of the tool itself. When this natural order of theory before fact is violated, the result is the "epistemological mystery" of education that Bruner laments (p. 65) in "The Growth of Mind": the emphasis on "extensiveness and coverage over intensiveness and depth." For Bruner (p. 16), education must parallel the structure of a discipline in order to preserve the relation of theory to fact, context to detail: "The disciplines of learning represent not only codified knowledge but ways of thought, habits of mind, implicit assumptions, short cuts, and styles of humor that never achieve explicit statement."

Gaff's (1983) assessment of general education suggests that the focus of such courses is essentially on what Bruner calls *codified knowledge*. Drawing on the work of Mayhew (1980), Gaff argues that the most common theory of teaching among university faculty is *covering the material*. This approach neglects what is equally or perhaps more important in higher education, helping students to understand and master intellectual method, so that they can reach their own conclusions and apply the methods to new situations. Teachers' insistence on covering content overrides students' needs for a broad understanding not just of what the discipline stands for, but also of its relation to other fields of study and other human problems.

When students in introductory courses fail — as they so often do — to understand these broad applications of a discipline, it may be because they are asked to accept the course content too absolutely. They fail to see that a discipline is primarily a dynamic, evolutionary process of inquiry — largely because it is not presented as such. Instead, they come to respond to the disciplines — and the whole of higher education — in much the same way one reacts to those trays of cellophane-wrapped tomatoes we find these days in large grocery stores. Something vital is lost when someone else does the selecting, arranging, weighing, and pricing. A good introductory course, as Robert McCauley maintains in Chapter Four, must help students to put means and ends, process and product in perspective. It is impossible to develop such a perspective when courses concentrate on ends to the exclusion of the ways of thinking, questions, and assumptions that generate them.

McCauley's concern for the relationship between means and ends, facts and theories is not new to discussions of education. Whitehead (1929, p. 2) began his discussion of the aims of education with an exhortation against inert ideas and an analysis of what he perceived as the fatal disconnection of subjects: "The result of teaching small parts of a large number of subjects is the passive reception of disconnected ideas, not illumined with any spark of vitality." Whitehead's comments identify a problem that a majority of institutions have yet to resolve: the absence of a core curriculum whose content and method introduce students adequately either to individual disciplines or to the meaning of higher education as a whole.

Although by many accounts general education is experiencing another national revival (see Gaff, 1983, for a summary of recent activity), the majority of schools rely heavily on a distribution system comprised largely of introductory courses. According to a 1981 survey by the Association of American Colleges (Gaff, 199–206) of 272 colleges and universities that had recently reviewed their general education programs, 80 percent of the new programs were discipline-based, presumably drawing on specified introductory courses across the curriculum. Eighty-eight percent of the programs included a breadth requirement that asked students to choose from a limited number of introductory courses in the humanities, sciences, and social sciences. Only 55 percent of the responding colleges included an interdisciplinary core course in their programs. This means that, in the newer general education programs, almost half of the students were relying on an array of unrelated introductory courses to achieve the goals of liberal education. In older programs, the figure is probably much higher. If faculty regard these courses as a pulpit from which to preach to the converted, it seems likely that neither the institution, nor the department, nor the students are being served very well.

Aside from faculty priorities that militate against a liberal approach to introductory courses, the evolution of the disciplines themselves exerts a strong pull toward specialization in the early courses. Dressel and Marcus (1982, p. 100) make the following observations about academic disciplines in relation to both research and learning: "As the disciplines have become more complex and esoteric in concepts, inquiry, modes, and use of abstractions, their relationships with specific objects, phenomena, problems, and actual behaviors have become less apparent. These connections between the abstract disci-

plines and complex realities have become unclear both to the practitioners of the discipline and to the public that supports disciplinary
study and research. . . . The fact that is so essential for teachers to grasp
is that as disciplines have been better defined, their purviews have been
so narrowed that 'real' problems of people and society can seldom be
understood or resolved by recourse to a single discipline."

Introductory courses, as Harriet Sheridan agrees, serve as an
essential liaison with the voters, taxpayers, legislators, corporate executives, and alumni contributors who pass through these courses as students and go on to make public policy and support or condemn higher
education. The proliferation of disciplines, fields, and specialized
research may be the bread and butter of the knowledge industry, but
the apparent removal of higher education from the social, economic,
moral, and political problems that make up daily life predisposes those
who take our introductory courses to view institutions and faculty of
higher education with impatience if not contempt.

Pedagogical Shortcomings

The teaching strategies used in introductory courses stem directly
from the conceptual framework that faculty adopt. Vast lecture halls,
grading based entirely on objective exams, teaching assistants who run
discussion sections to answer the questions that students never have all
testify to the underlying philosophy that the introductory course is an
exercise in memorization. In Chapter Eight, John Southin considers
the implications of the coverage problem for students' misperceptions of
the dynamic nature of science. He concludes that introductory courses
should undertake less to cover a field than to uncover parts that represent the whole. However, as the authors of both Chapters Two and
Four argue, this pedagogical approach is impossible until we change
our guiding metaphors about teaching. We must abandon the familiar
notion of mind as storage compartment and of education as input.

The coverage approach has some disturbing long-range implications as well. Students learn more than data from introductory
courses. In these formative experiences, they learn what it is to be a
student, what is required to get by, what it means to acquire an edu-
tion, and whether college is anything more than acquiring job certifi-
cation. If faculty in upper-division courses are impatient with students'
reluctance to ask original questions, find novel solutions, use what we
assume they already know, or examine their own preconeptions, they
may be witnessing the outcome of that initial college experience. If students are taught, albeit implicitly, to be passive seekers and transcribers

of information, that is what they become. Further, they set their sights accordingly in subsequent courses, often actively resisting our attempts in upper-division courses to get them to go beyond the information that we give them. In Chapter Three, Robert Dunham and Maryellen Gleason explore this problem in some detail and suggest alternatives that focus on changes in roles for faculty and students.

Yet another factor that affects the teaching of introductory courses deserves attention: economics. Introductory courses are usually big money-makers for a department, because the most students are typically taught by the least-prepared faculty: teaching assistants, adjunct faculty, untenured assistant professors, and senior faculty who are not adroit enough to sidestep the assignment. Maintaining such a collection of ancillary staff—Booth (1983) calls them "hopeless hirelings"—is attractive to administrators, who can process the most students for the least amount of money. However, the economic temptations have an important bearing on course quality. Lacking any ties to the business of either the department or the institution, this fringe group of faculty tends to miss out on opportunities for informal collegial exchanges and to be excluded from the faculty development activities that a department, college, or university sponsors. In the absence of a professional nucleus for the development of these courses, they tend to epitomize the worst of teaching at any level: the tendency to model teaching practices on one's own experience as a student.

That this tendency exerts considerable influence on the pedagogy of introductory courses is borne out in many chapters of this volume. Introductory courses and large enrollments seem to be linked as inextricably as the bell and food in Pavlov's conditioning experiments. The disinclination of faculty to teach these courses, combined with the economics of size and the large number of students processed through them, seems to render the size issue an inescapable fact of life. McCauley's novel suggestion—that, if we must have large classes, we should put them in the upper division, where students have already learned something about working independently—challenges us to examine our preconceptions about the structuring and teaching of introductory courses and to question the status quo.

Rethinking Introductory Courses

All the chapters in this volume agree that what can be termed the higher goals of learning are necessary for the introductory course. For the most part, however, all the contributors remain rather closely identified with a particular discipline. The problems of introductory courses span the disciplines. Many of the solutions offered here do not. If, as I have suggested, the shortcomings of introductory courses derive on the one hand from the very structure of our disciplines and on the other from our historic inability or disinclination to incorporate the higher goals into lower-level classes, one last perspective is worth considering: the development of introductory courses based not in disciplines and departments but in academic areas. Turner's (1977, p. 75) rationale for interdisciplinary study in the social sciences is appropriate for the curriculum in general: "My suggestion is that, instead of working in blinders, anthropologists and scholars in adjacent disciplines interested in cross-cultural problems should make an earnest. . . attempt at mutual empathy—earnest in the sense that various anthropological perspectives, hybrids such as ethnography, and fields such as the sociology of knowledge, and significant others, might be treated at least as a unified field whose unity might have something to do with the systems theory view that there are systems and systemic relations so fundamental that they occur in many different living and even inorganic phenomena." Models of this sort already exist: Brown University's "modes of thought" group with courses in humanities, natural science, social studies, and formal thought; the University of Michigan's course in approaches to knowledge (analytic, empirical, moral, esthetic); Bradford College's new core program derived from the curriculum proposed by Boyer and Levine (1981).

In one sense, the development of interdisciplinary introductions is anachronistic—a throwback (at least from an organizational standpoint) to the early structure of American universities. For example, in 1767 Harvard had four departments: Greek, logic and metaphysics, mathematics, and natural philosophy. The simplicity of such organization provides an intellectual center that otherwise seems so elusive for faculty and students alike, making it virtually impossible not to come to terms with the fundamental questions that concern human beings and the ways in which intelligent people go about answering them. Halliburton's (1981) discussion of interdisciplinary studies expresses what may be a logical extension of the points of view argued here. He concludes (p. 470) that "an applied, interdisciplinary, general education approach can develop in learners a flexibility and depth that finally do more real human good than the narrower education toward which we have been drifting." If, as the writers here suggest, the goals of the introductory course must transcend the discipline itself, interdisciplinary introductory courses may begin to rescue students and curriculum from the perils of too much information about too little.

9

References

Ausubel, D. "Cognitive Structure and Transfer." In N. Entwistle and D. Hounsell (Eds.), *How Students Learn*. Readings in Higher Education 1. Lancaster, England: Institute for Research and Development in Post-Compulsory Education, University of Lancaster, 1975.

Booth, W. "Presidential Address: Arts and Scandals 1982." *PMLA*, 1983, *98*, 312–322.

Boyer, E., and Levine, A. *A Quest for Common Learning*. Washington, D.C.: Carnegie Foundation for the Advancement of Teaching, 1981.

Bruner, J. *The Relevance of Education*. (2nd ed.) New York: Norton, 1973.

Carnegie Foundation for the Advancement of Teaching. *Missions of the College Curriculum: A Contemporary Review with Suggestions*. San Francisco: Jossey-Bass, 1977.

Dressel, P. L., and Marcus, D. *On Teaching and Learning in College: Reemphasizing the Roles of Learners and the Disciplines in Liberal Education*. San Francisco: Jossey-Bass, 1982.

Gaff, J. G. *General Education Today: A Critical Analysis of Controversies, Practices, and Reforms*. San Francisco: Jossey-Bass, 1983.

Gamson, Z., and Associates. *Liberating Education*. San Francisco: Jossey-Bass, 1984.

Halliburton, D. "Interdisciplinary Studies." In A. W. Chickering and Associates, *The Modern American College: Responding to the New Realities of Diverse Students and a Changing Society*. San Francisco: Jossey-Bass, 1981.

Mayhew, L. *General Education and the Metatheory of the Course*. Teaching Resources Center Monograph 10. Davis: University of California, 1980.

Turner, V. "Process, System, and Symbol: A New Anthropological Synthesis." *Daedalus*, 1977, *196* (3), 61–80.

Whitehead, A. N. *The Aims of Education and Other Essays*. New York: Macmillan, 1929.

Karen I. Spear is associate dean of liberal education and assistant professor of English at the University of Utah, Salt Lake City.

PART 1.

The Crisis in Teaching
Introductory Courses

Senior faculty are the best prepared to remedy the assorted illiteracies and cognitive deficiencies of today's beginning students, although they typically choose to have little direct contact with these students.

Where Have All the Senior Faculty Gone?

Harriet W. Sheridan

Although the most difficult courses to teach are courses on the introductory level, few experienced university faculty teach them. At some institutions, almost all the general education curriculum is taught by graduate teaching assistants, who are sometimes supervised carefully by senior faculty and sometimes not. Senior faculty undertake the lectures for large courses, for which prepackaged, commercially vended notes may be made avilable, but it is the graduate students who lead discussion sections and grade the written work. Yet, it is in discussion and in writing that students engage in real learning.

In his presidential address to the Modern Language Association, Wayne Booth (1983, p. 319) spoke sharply to the point of professional abdication: "Not only are most of our beginning students taught by beginners who are given impossible teaching loads and paid one half to one third what beginning assistant professors are paid. We have compounded the felony by providing for those beginners no orientation, little or no in-service supervision or exchange with experienced teachers, and no hope for any recognition for a job well done.... [We] need no market research to reveal that most of the students who pass through the courses taught by these vast staffs of hopeless hirelings are

K. I. Spear (Ed.). *Rejuvenating Introductory Courses.* New Directions for Teaching and Learning, no. 20. San Francisco: Jossey-Bass, December 1984.

at best puzzled and bored. Often they are angry. They think of themselves as victims of a meaningless requirement, rightly determined to get the hurdle 'out of the way,' as their advisors obligingly put it to them."

From Excitement to Resignation: The Metamorphosis
of the Freshman Class

Each fall, our campuses receive entering freshmen with the usual bureaucratic welcome, lining them up to register and purchase textbooks, assigning them numbers, enrolling them in required courses, talking at them about the values of a liberal education, and haranguing them about the deadliest sin, plagiarism. Little by little, their innocent hopefulness wanes, their expectations of receiving the key to all mythologies fades, and they either jostle in the company of the competers and the me-firsters or resign themselves to average grades and dim futures. "Shades of the prison house begin to close upon the growing boy." If there is anything left of the "vision splendid" in the freshman's baggage, it soon fades.

The excitement, even euphoria, that pervades the freshman classroom at first is a phenomenon that repeats every year. Pleasure at being in the university, free of parental constraints, and on the verge of learning important and useful things at last overpowers freshmen's anxiety about being found to be not as good as everyone thought them and their brooding suspicion that no one will ever learn to love them. But it does not take long for excitement to dwindle into resignation as new students find themselves in classes so large that even the section leader fails to learn their names, scarcely able to see the features of the lecturer in front at the podium; or else gathered in front of a videotape screen set up at another hour in order to accommodate the overflow. "A great lecturer," concludes the freshman, "but nobody knows or cares about what I understand and how I respond."

Or, they may find themselves on the departmental playing fields where careers are ultimately fostered or thwarted: Science courses are used to screen out those who will become mere citizens and consumers from the premeds who are going to make it or the few who will go on to specialize in the field and take a higher degree — 10 percent or less at most institutions. Almost all will find themselves in composition courses, that are taught by the disinclined, and in foreign language courses, required once again but probably not taught any better than they were when they were jettisoned in the sixties, that have been anathematized for their tedium and irrelevance.

Disinclined Faculty

What students make of the freshman year finally is a rite of passage into sophomore slump. What we the professoriate make of it is a professional disgrace. Since most of the students we teach in our introductory courses will never become classroom theorists like us but will instead go on to become mere practitioners—journalists, parents, business executives, computer programmers, lawyers, public service volunteers, senators, and presidents—we do not regard the teaching of such courses as sufficiently dignified or rewarding for senior faculaty, so we turn the field over to underpaid "hopeless hirelings" who, fortunately for our institutions, succeed in teaching better than we have any right to expect.

Yet, introductory courses furnish the professoriate with a challenging and important task, one that requires both the knowledge of scholarship and the wisdom of experience. What is called for is such familiarity and ease with the field of learning that it can readily be shaped and translated for the novice, who wants to learn not only the content of the subject but also something about where and how it came to be a field of study, its underlying values and assumptions, its typical methodologies, and its connections with other fields of study and with experience. All these things do not necessarily have to be taken up in each course, but when any of them are, the subject takes on special vitality. Clearly, the task is one for the master teacher, not the neophyte.

Underprepared Students

Yet, the complexities of teaching the nonspecialist in general education courses must appear even greater when the second half of the equation, the condition of the student, is factored in. The intellectual background of most entering freshmen today was prophetically described in the fourteenth century by the poet Geoffrey Chaucer in an early epistemological work, "The House of Fame." In this poem, the narrator dreams that he emerges from the Temple of Venus, on the walls of which the whole history of Troy has been depicted, including the legend of Dido and Aeneas. Passing through a wicket gate, somewhat like Alice going through the little door in Wonderland, he enters a large field, which is described as being without town, or house, or tree, or bush, or grass, or plowed land—for all the field, the poet tells us, was composed only of fine sand, like the Desert of Libya. Nothing of human creation was visible to him no matter where he looked. "Oh Christ that art in bliss," the dreamer cries, "from phantom and illusion save me."

In the Temple of Venus, the narrator takes delight in the so-called historical facts of man's existence, even if these facts in their distorted state add up to a sad testimony about human character. The guiding principle is that *any* facts will be welcome, rather than none at all. When the narrator emerged from the Temple, he discovered himself to be in a wasteland of the imagination; it required divine intervention to rescue him from this plight.

I take the Desert of Libya as the emblem for the state of cultural literacy of the students now coming into higher education. Survey after survey documents students' deficiencies. They do not know geography. They know little or nothing about any other country's language or history and not much more about their own. English has become a foreign language. They cannot make graphs or charts. Science education is in dire straits. Most freshmen entering New Jersey public colleges fail basic algebra tests. The whole American educational system, critically appraised in *A Nation at Risk,* Boyer's *High School,* Goodlad's *A Place Called School,* Sizer's *Horace's Compromise,* and others, has been described by journalists as "a spreading desert strewn with potholes."

Of course, such complaints are periodic in our national history. Often, they are preludes to self-congratulatory posturings that conceal snobbery. Worse, they are products of an ideology that has waited patiently for the sixties to end so that students may once again be pressed back into obligatory curricula — a retreat to the past and its basics that is claimed to be the only solution to problems of national verbal and scientific illiteracy.

Too much has changed environmentally for such a retreat to be valid. Forty years ago, Ortega y Gasset (1944, p. 38) observed that "the new barbarian is above all the professional man, more learned than ever before but at the same time more uncultured." What was true then is even more true now. The cultural desert from which our students currently emerge, television-sophisticated as they are about artifacts of violence and sex, has left them deprived of knowledge of the history and created works of humankind, deaf to textual allusions and contextual meanings, and made uneasy by the claims that solitary contemplation makes on the imagination. They have been surrendered to the easy enjoyment of popular culture, which provides its own neatly packaged beginning, middle, and end, usually at high volume. "The dramatic resources of video seem permanently suited to imaginations of desire that are relatively passive, relatively frozen by the pre-imagings of the makers, relatively resistant to reflection and reconsideration" (Booth, 1982, p. 51). During a recent television talk show that devoted ten minutes to a discussion of the *Reader's Digest* condensed Bible, three clergymen—Protestant, Catholic, and Jewish—expressed their regret about the distortions and oversimplifications of the condensation. They were abruptly silenced by their host, who broke in and said truculently, "But, the Bible is really rather hard reading, isn't it?" If beginning students lack imagination and sensitivity to meaning, it may result in part from the models provided by the television gurus responsible for mediating public discussion of issues.

When I first began teaching, I made it a practice to ask my freshmen to list the books they had read during their high school years that had impressed and moved them. Predictably, such class texts as *Julius Caesar* and *A Tale of Two Cities* and such teenage cult texts as *The Catcher in the Rye* and *Steppenwolf* turned up as constant choices. But, when I once again put the question after a hiatus of several decades, no one text was named. Instead, students named a cartoon character, Garfield the cat, represented on the *New York Times* list of trade best sellers by not one but four books—slightly more than a quarter of the list.

In sum, although the schools must bear their share of responsibility for failing to stir and maintain students' intellectual curiosity, the mechanisms for easy and passive gratification that litter our cultural landscape make this task more difficult than it has ever been before The current state of literacy has been influenced by both pedagogical and media-directed simplifications of intellectual and esthetic processes to the mechanistic, specialized, quantifiable, and saleable. These influences have been abetted by the disinclination to require arduous intellectual work during the early formative years of a student's education.

Teaching Today's Students

It is crucial for faculties to recognize that the habits of an earlier period that organized intellect and emotion, that gave us the means to epitomize and articulate ideas and feelings, and that provided our texts and contexts—the habits that most faculty developed and matured—are far less present today. Yet, many of us still operate on the assumption that these habits continue to exercise their historical force, and we are thereby doomed to disappointment and misunderstanding, even failure, in our work with our students.

Senior faculty became faculty because they were bookish and grew up valuing the texts and traditions of the past—the printed word, the dissemination of recorded information, the hypothesis patiently validated again and again before it is accepted as fact. The materials and techniques of the rational process must each year be transmitted afresh to the new students who throng our classrooms.

The Necessity of Writing

During the fifties and early sixties, as a result of the example set to his colleagues in the English Department at Carleton College by Scott Elledge, now professor emeritus of Cornell University, devoted teacher and productive scholar of the Renaissance, we all, junior and senior faculty alike, learned about the challenges and rewards of teaching introduction-to-literature courses and freshman composition.

At the heart of the educational experience for all students, whether they concentrate in science, social science, business, engineering, or the arts or choose to major in the humanities, must be the critical expression of ideas and opinions in writing. Whatever else the content of introductory courses may be, reading and writing are its center. Students who glide through such courses without ever having to grapple with the meaning of texts or having their own writing read carefully and subsequently revised and resubmitted have been cheated by a professoriate that cannot excuse its dereliction by claiming practical impossibility. Later in this chapter, I will describe some strategies for accomplishing such teaching for large numbers of students.

Literate writers on the college level—that is, writers who can see beyond their own response to stimuli or who can respond rather than parrot—are experienced readers. But, with the amount of reading that students do outside the academy decreasing, we must increase the emphasis on this function within its walls. If our students are made neither full by reading nor exact by writing, they are not well prepared for a world of accelerated change, increasingly complex technology, cultural commercialization, and ethical confrontations undreamed of by the generations that preceded us.

Students who are expected to write ought to be asked to write about something that requires more than mere repetition. But, what can their topics be? They derive what they know and can write about from two sources: from printed texts that should be pondered, reread, analyzed, and translated into comprehensible, integrated terms and from experience that they rarely ponder and even more rarely understand.

There is no single source of curricular experience from which students can be expected to derive the organizing faculties that lead both to intellectual strength and cultural apprehension and to the content for the papers that they write. Of course, many sources of intellectual stimulation lie in the worlds that students inhabit after class. What I am asking of introductory courses is that they each require some writing that calls for active, thoughtful responsiveness to something to be learned and that is read and responded to by a faculty member who is interested in discovering whether learning has taken place — an objective that surely is central to the commitment of the professional teacher.

It is true that more insight and imagination lie beneath the superficial irregularities of our students' writing than we sometimes given them credit for, as Mina Shaughnessy (1977) has convincingly demonstrated. They know more than they seem to, and they can respond in more complicated ways than their command of language seems at first to allow. Yet, when we first begin to ask our students to write, it is at a point when they have yet to enter their specialized studies of literature, history, the classics, science, anthropology, psychology — any of the fields that incrementally build up connections between what they know and the past, their own world, and the future. Thus, we need early on to put them in touch with the eclectic cultural connections that will allow them to organize and stabilize their thoughts and opinions in a coherent, not random, way. If such an imperative is consciously performed, it is likely to make every course a history course in part and to provide every subject with connections between the specifics of the discipline and the rational and cultural processes that give it its shape or organization and govern its future. In effect, we demonstrate to our students that what we now think we know was not always known, that it came to pass through human intervention, and that it will alter or be replaced by the same means.

Ronald Berman (1982, p. 80), former chairman of the National Endowment for the Humanities, has offered the thesis that in essence every course is in part a remedial course. As therapy for perceived cultural illiteracy, he reports (p. 79) that he dots lectures with the names of books and critics: "I have each class keep a running list of these allusions, and I keep books in my office to lend. I make an effort to place books in their historical periods, although this takes away a lot of time that might be used for study of the text. I note also that these are the most popular classes, the students feeling evidently that they are getting a return not previously paid on their investment. The simple provision of historical information, or that about writing, fills a large and empty space. Allusiveness is good for the soul of the instructor since it may so easily be mistaken for intelligence. . . . There is eventually a point of no return in education, for which remedial teaching is useless. It takes a number of courses and several years to provide basic information about history and writing — anything less is emptying the ocean by buckets." However, Berman also sounds a warning note about the allusive method — that is to say, about the broadening and thickening of discourse by reference to ideas, scholarly progress over the years, historical context, and common experience. He observes that students intent on passing the course with as high a grade as possible want to get on with it and become resentful about allusions, craving the immediate conversion of study into a unit of course credit. In this age of anxiety, our students bring to campus a concern for the future that is expressed as a tropism toward the practical and a hunger for competitive advantage.

In a valuable little text produced to help college and high school students get a basic understanding of the methods and purposes of college work, Jack W. Meiland (1981, p. 1) reports "Many college students and college graduates—including some very bright and serious people—have told me that it took them several years of college before they finally realized what kind of work was expected of them and what faculty was trying to teach them. Perhaps if someone had taken these students aside and had tried to explain the nature of college work to them—even had merely given them a few hints—they would not have felt so confused, so much at sea, and they might have used their college years more effectively."

When I have asked colleagues in various disciplines to name the most serious defects in the written work of their upper-division students, they have singled out students' lack of skill in organizing and developing ideas, which I take to be the result of lack of practice in thinking a thought through from beginning to end, and in presenting and defending ideas before a critical audience. Faculty seem to assume that, by the time students reach campus, they have become experienced in constructing an argument, they have learned to suspend belief until all the facts are in, they can anticipate and respond to objections to their own position, and they are able to identify the assumptions and biases that underlie any expression of views. In short, we assume that they have learned to think.

I believe that we are guilty of assuming more than experience allows us to. Recently, in the course of teaching an essay by the historian Edward Hallett Carr (1980, p. 103) to a group of twenty-two freshmen, I asked the students to write a couple of paragraphs explicating the meaning of Carr's statement, "The predicament of the historian is a reflection of the nature of man." The two passages that follow show one student's painful struggle with Carr's rather provocative comparison, a struggle resulting from the student's failure to understand the key term *predicament*. In both drafts, the weaknesses in thinking may come down to the seemingly simple yet complex matter of dealing with words precisely—or in pedagogical terms, of vocabulary recognition.

> In this statement Carr is drawing a comparison between the predicament of the historian and the nature of man. The predicament of the historian is manifold. The historian does not merely record the facts. He must put the facts in perspective

with modern thought. Only then will the facts take on some meaning and have some relevance in the time in which they are displayed. Also, the historian must interpret the facts. A whole fact might not be important as it stands in its original form. The historian must select which part of the fact to bring out and which part or parts to suppress. To understand Carr's statement we must also understand the nature of man as it relates to this particular theme. Man is a product of his era, and therefore his nature will be shaped by the time in which he lives. We must realize that when compared to all of time, man has a very narrow perspective of life and his species' own inherent nature. Carr's intention to compare man and the historian is shown by the statement: "The relation of man to his environment is the relation of the historian to his theme." Man is neither the subject of his environment nor its ruler. In the same manner the historian is not the slave of his facts nor their master. Both man and the historian must participate in a give and take relationship with either their environment, for man, or the facts, for the historian. To an extent, both groups can control and therefore shape their objects into their final form. Another comparison that can be drawn is that both man and the historian have a limited frame of reference due to the time in which they live. The historian cannot know how ancient man thought of the facts that today are called history. Along the same lines, man does not know if his present nature has always been as it is, or if man was a different creature altogether many years ago. It is true that the predicament of the historian and the nature of man have points in common. However, we must always remember that every historian is a man, and therefore Carr's original statement "the predicament of the historian is a reflection of the nature of man," will hold true forever. (First draft)

Man is constantly in a predicament. He is continually trying to obtain a better understanding of his universe. This universe, however, is constantly changing around him. Therein lies the predicament. In trying to understand his present universe man takes empirical truths, based on experience and observation, and forms theories which fit his known facts. His desire to be master of his facts reflects his desire to control his environment. By forming tenable theories man feels as if he is controlling his universe. The historian is caught in the same predicament of adapting his theories to fit a changing world. Proper selection and presentation of the facts will shape them into a body of knowledge comprehensible to his present day society. By shaping the facts into a relevant collection of knowledge, the historian has partially achieved temporary control of his facts and his universe. This control is only temporary because as society and man change, so must the historian's theories. (Third draft)

Despite the tighter organization of the third draft, the student's exposition is still weakened by his insecure understanding of a key term. I learned from this to take nothing for granted, not even a bright student's level of vocabulary recognition. And, the initiation of vocabulary drills designed to improve the user's lexicon at the start of each class meeting proved to be a pleasant novelty for the class as a whole.

Rewarding Senior Faculty

My theme thus far has been that teaching introductory courses is a difficult business that calls on the talents of the most seasoned teachers and versatile scholars. Its intellectual objectives are so fundamental to the success of the educational process that colleges of stature must be willing to commit their senior faculty resources to this enterprise. But, the rewards for such service are rare. Both the administration and the professoriate have placed little value on contributions to the success of the early curriculum. Teaching introductory courses is not easy. It can be maddening to have to become more and more elementary as students come to higher education knowing less and less. Reading student writing is not the most gripping of intellectual challenges, and correcting student writing becomes an exercise in self-control. It is much easier to go off to one's carrel in the library and prepare a lecture in one's field of specialization than it is to keep office hours for those whom we regard as the bumptious, the timid, the naive, and the ignorant — heedless of the reality that they will become contributors to the alumni fund and supporters of educational tax appropriations.

To complicate the task, I think that introductory courses should serve yet another function, one that goes against the grain of the traditional scholarly life, which emphasizes independence and solitariness. It seems to me important to introduce students as soon as possible to the collaborative way of life that pervades the world outside the academy. By this I mean that the development of early opportunities for students to work together on common learning projects initiates them into the role of active audience, of giver as well as taker, and starts a process that should extend through their careers.

The Undergraduate Writing Fellows Program, directed by Tori

23

Haring-Smith of the English department at Brown University, is one of the most successful collaborative ventures at that institution. It puts upperclassmen from all fields of concentration who have been selected for their writing skill and prepared in a special course on the teaching of writing into introductory courses across the curriculum to serve as the first readers of student writing, pointing out surface errors and responding to obscurities and misorganization. When students give the final draft to the faculty member, they also hand in the other drafts. This strategy has been lauded by the students being served; by the writing fellows, who have learned that you have to know something in order to teach it; and by the faculty, who now feel free to make writing assignments in courses with 400 students.

A comparable collaborative arrangement has been initiated in beginning foreign language courses, under the direction of William Crossgrove of the German department. Under this arrangement, students returned from foreign study serve as classroom resources. Some other forms of academic collaborative involvement put students and faculty together to revise courses (the Odyssey Program, supported by a grant from the Fund for the Improvement of Post-Secondary Education and administered by Karen Romer) and to observe teaching in introductory nondepartmental courses at the request of junior faculty (the Lilly Post-Doctoral Teaching Fellowship Program, administered by Carey McIntosh).

Brown has now crossed over the threshold of collaborative learning ventures into the wide field of opportunities waiting for development. Our dominant principle is that students learn best by active participation and grow by active contribution to one another's growth. Our terrain will be chiefly introductory courses. Bringing the students' right to know and to learn how to use the tools of learning into harmonious relationship with society's need for graduates who can surrender individual rights for the common good will prove no easy task.

I am not sure how many crises in education the American public will experience before its members begin to think unkindly of the academic profession to which the task has been entrusted. It would be reassuring to see senior faculty back in the classroom doing the other half of their job as cheerfully and competently as they have done their scholarship.

References

Berman, R. "Shakespeare as Remedial Reading." *Commentary*, 1982, *73*, 79–81.
Booth, W. "The Company We Keep: Self-Making in Imaginative Art, Old and New." *Daedalus*, 1982, *112*, 51.
Booth, W. "Presidential Address: Arts and Scandals 1982." *PMLA*, 1983, *98*, 312–322.

24

Carr, E. H. "The Histories of the Facts," from *What Is History?* In A. Eastman (Ed.), *The Norton Reader.* (5th ed.) New York: Norton, 1980.

Meiland, J. W. *College Thinking: How to Get the Best out of College.* New York: New American Library, 1981.

Ortega y Gasset, J. *Mission of the University.* Princeton, N.J.: Princeton University Press, 1944.

Shaughnessy, M. *Errors and Expectations: A Guide for the Teacher of Basic Writing.* New York: Oxford University Press, 1977.

Harriet W. Sheridan is dean of the college and professor of English at Brown University.

The proper aims and character of introductory courses can only be discovered within the context of discussion about the proper aims and character of education as a whole.

What Should Introductory Courses Do?

Marshall W. Gregory

The term *introductory courses* is perhaps unfortunate, for *introductory* is often used in a depreciatory sense. Insofar as it implies that *introductory* courses are more superficial or less substantial than *advanced* courses, it masks the truth that students find their introductory courses harder to master—because they are novices—than upper-level courses later on. Students are always more vulnerable to failure, either perceived or real, in the initial stages of learning than they are after having been seasoned by experience. Moreover, the depreciatory view of introductory courses also masks the truth that introductions to disciplines—as to people—often create indelible impressions that delight or disgust and attract or repel. The tone of an introduction can have everything to do with the way a relationship subsequently develops between one person and another or between students and disciplines. But introductory courses do not merely introduce disciplines; they introduce all of higher education.

Freshmen and sophomores do not learn only about English, history, or economics; they learn about college as a whole. They learn to read the ethos of their academic community the same way one learns to read the ethos of one's own family, congregation, or neighborhood.

K. I. Spear (Ed.). *Rejuvenating Introductory Courses.* New Directions for Teaching and Learning, no. 20. San Francisco: Jossey-Bass, December 1984.

They sense, even if they cannot articulate, assumptions about the educational enterprise that are held by their teachers and administrators. Insofar as those teachers and administrators reflect assumptions held by legislators, educational critics, professional unions, and the general public, it follows that these courses are introductory in a more profound and pervasive sense than is usually discussed. It is thus impossible to talk about the aims or character of introductory college courses without viewing them in the context of the aims and character of higher education as a whole. If we can get a picture of what to approve of and disapprove of among the attitudes and assumptions held about education in general, we may be in a better position to say what should be done with introductory courses.

Career Education Versus Liberal Education

As recently as twenty-five years ago few college students declared their majors until the end of the sophomore or beginning of the junior year. The first two years of college education were usually thought of by teachers and students alike as an introduction to general education. However vaguely that introduction might have been defined, most people agreed that a genuine education should begin with it. Now, however, high school seniors declare their majors on their college application forms, and freshmen are no longer given the luxury of taking their first two years of college to decide on possible careers. The insistence that they begin making vocational choices starts sitting on them like an incubus as early as junior high school. Thus the minds of most college students are fixed on careers from the moment they enter the college corridors.

Two important consequences have been created by this narrowed definition of a college education. First, students who are misadvised to make premature choices about life-long vocational goals often wind up either clumsily changing their majors during their last two years, or, worse, going into jobs they hate because college has led them to think about careers only in terms of income levels, retirement plans, and advancement opportunities, not in terms of intellectual growth, emotional rewards, or social contributions. Second, as colleges and universities increasingly accept the impoverished aim of merely providing career training, they fail to help students clarify the value judgments that must underlie all satisfying job choices. Equally important, colleges also fail to help students develop the critical intelligence that will ultimately allow them to control their jobs instead of being controlled by them. In short, the distinction between liberal and vocational education has all but disappeared in American education. Only in grades one through six can one count on finding the liberal arts of reading, writing, speaking, listening, analyzing, criticizing, and appreciating consistently taught in a disinterested way: taught simply for the sake of the students' own growth and development as human beings. At every other academic level the trend these days is either to teach these activities as isolatable "skills" worth learning because one's chosen career — or the next step in the educational ladder — requires them, or not to teach them at all.

The outside cultural forces that oppose liberal education have long been identified and discussed — consumerism, acquisitiveness, status seeking, relativism, specialization, materialism, and so on — but the forces that work against liberal education within academe are harder to identify and less seldom discussed. Three of the most damaging are a chaotic confusion about means and ends, a vitiating refusal to discuss moral issues — especially the ethics of professionalism and teaching, and a crippling subservience to mechanical metaphors.

Confusion About Means and Ends

The prevalence of vocationalism in American colleges and universities is not solely a product of external cultural pressures. Those people outside academe who would reduce all education, whether they realize it or not, to mere skills training, set the trends and form the character of higher education not because their views and arguments are intrinsically irresistible, but because confusions within academe create a vacuum. Academe's opposition to the many powerful forces pushing it into vocationalism tends to be querulous and defeatist, not authoritative or vigorous. We do a lot of hand-wringing but not much table-pounding. Our support of liberal education is rich in platitudes but poor in arguments. Platitudes predictably appear in the opening paragraphs of most college catalogues and in the closing paragraphs of most commencement speeches, but arguments hardly appear anywhere. Where vital arguments *do* appear is mainly in discussions of means, not ends: the technology of how to do things, not the debate about which things are most worth doing. Schools of education, for example, with their sometimes vast resources of faculty and funding, could do much more to foment vital philosophical discussion about educational ends. But, lured by the same rainbow's-end dream that has deluded the social sciences generally — the pursuit of "scientific" predictability and control — schools of education settle mainly for research about means, not discussion about ends. But they are not alone in this short-sightedness, and, in any event, their failures do not excuse those whose support for liberal education consists mainly of hauling out platitudes about ends the same way old soldiers haul out their dress uniforms: as costumes to be worn on ceremonial occasions that bow to tradition but do not set policy.

The real end of education is to cultivate the life of the mind and to make the advantages of that cultivation available to both individuals and to society. This does not mean that career training must be abandoned, but it does mean that education should never be reduced to career training alone. There is much cant these days that a liberal education is too idealistic, ivory towerish, just plain impractical, or, worst of all, elitist. The problem with this cant is the problem with all cant: It substitutes clichés for thoughtfulness and pretends to superior thoughtfulness while doing so. Those who talk this way simply ignore the personal and social catastrophes that will fall on the modern world if the cultivation of the mind ceases, or they simply beg the question of how the mind's cultivation is to be accomplished if higher education gives up the task. All of those arts on which modern survival depends — such as science, politics, the production and distribution of economic goods, urban design, international diplomacy, population control, and agricultural production — must keep a pace of improvement and effectiveness that matches the pace of our ever-increasing problems. These are only the arts on which we depend for our physical survival. When we talk about what we need to ensure our spiritual survival as well, then it is clear that other arts must be included in our list as well. Both the fine arts and the arts of different kinds of thinking and speculation — religious, philosophical, and ethical, for example — must also be cultivated. What happens when they are not cultivated is that people, and the societies they make up, can no longer live deliberately. They lose the power of making choices about their individual or collective destiny; they become the victims of whatever influences get to them first or whatever groups happen to have the most muscle. This catastrophe happens when people cease *thinking*. Real thought — the hard work of seeking out causes, comparing alternative lines of actions, forecasting consequences, evaluating moral effects, making rational arguments for and against positions, and so on — may occasionally bloom in an isolated genius but can have little effect on a whole society unless it is cultivated and embedded in a tradition that possesses some degree of credence and authority throughout society generally.

Where else except in institutions of education may a tradition of developed, systematic, and rational thought be cultivated? This tradition includes time-tested modes of inquiry, bodies of knowledge, systematic approaches, the freedom to pursue paths that may terminate in dead ends, and freedom from political or parochial controls. Educational institutions are the only institutions we have with the requisite traditions, apparatus, vocabularies, and interest in the life of the mind as a whole. Cultivating that life means providing an arena where both teachers and students find themselves stimulated to expand their powers of criticism, imagination, and independence.

These are precisely the powers that education sacrifices, however, when it turns into exclusive or even predominant career training. Education for careers means fitting and trimming students' abilities to fit preset molds. It does not empower them to improve old molds, to dream up new and better ones, or to challenge the authority of molds altogether. The readiness with which academics have agreed to become accomplices in the fitting and trimming of students' powers reveals enormous confusions among us about means and ends. Academic diplomas often have little purpose beyond giving a patina of credentialing, as it is now called (the nineteenth century term was *genteel respectability*) to uncritical conformity.

The basic reason for inquiring into what we want is that we make up our individual and collective lives as we go along. If we are not to be disappointed with what we get, we have to be clear about what we want. Modern wisdom has it that human beings are determined by many different forces — their genes, their early upbringing, their traumas, and so on — but the truth contained in this view has been so exaggerated and overemphasized that people sometimes act as if they have no power of choice about anything. This is a seductive view, for it promises to relieve us of moral responsibility for our actions. But it is also a false view. As long as we can see alternatives and forecast consequences, we have the power to choose one idea, one attitude, or one line of action. The deterministic factors we live with may sometimes make choice extremely difficult, but they can never erase choice altogether. The most dangerous prospect for a society is when people give up their power of choice because they cease believing in it, a fate literally worse than death. In a society where this event occurs life can become nightmarish. The only effective preventative is the cultivation of the life of the mind. Whatever defects universities and colleges exhibit, this cultivation is the soul of their existence.

Universities and colleges cannot cultivate the life of the mind, however, unless they maintain their own intellectual independence. The business of physics and English courses is physics and English, but a university's business is criticism: Matthew Arnold's "free play of the mind on all subjects." The business of higher education is neither automatically to reinforce the values and prejudices of society in general nor automatically to challenge them, but to create a community dedi-cated to developing rational responses to them. Genuine criticism is the attempt to view the values of culture not from a local perspective but from a universal, timeless, classless, and rational perspective. Unless we are attempting to acquire such a perspective, we have no criterion for progress or truth except our own self-interest. While some people actually talk as if human beings would be better off if they simply accepted the inescapable subjectivity of all value judgments, no one would ever choose, once the consequences were clearly seen, to live in a world where everyone's notions of progress and truth were synonymous with self-interest. While conceding, then, that the perspective demanded by criticism is the hardest perspective in the world to achieve and that none of us ever achieves it perfectly, the truth remains that it is the only perspective that will correct our prejudices and liberate us to see new possibilities. This is the business of criticism and criticism is the busi-ness of the university. But unless we *know* that this is our business, unless we can articulate and agree about ends, our means will be a col-lection of unrelated and largely ignored introductory courses. As these courses mechanically stamp out students like license plates, the bulk of our attention goes to specific courses in the major, which are increas-ingly organized to serve vocational ends. At that point, "the idea of a university," to use Cardinal Newman's phrase, will cease being an idea at all, for universities will have lost their independent informing prin-ciples. They will simply have become enormous machines for grinding out vast quantities of smaller machines called "qualified graduates."

The Ethics of Professionalism and Teaching

A second force working against liberal education within aca-deme, and therefore working against introductory courses that educate as well as introduce, is our steady refusal to discuss ethical issues, espe-cially the ethical implications of professionalism and teaching. Educa-tion has become a marketable commodity in this country. Almost half the high school graduates in America go on to some form of higher edu-cation while millions who have been out of high school for years are entering college. This makes education a major cultural force in society like television, religion, pop music, credit cards, and professional sports. Millions of people are embracing our programs, our textbooks, and our classrooms. As they do so they ingest the prevailing attitudes and values that our culture holds about education.

Complicated and vast as this issue is, academics do very little to clarify it. We seem to take for granted that the effects of our programs and activities always come down on the side of truth, justice, and morality (not to mention the American way) and therefore do not need the same kind of hard scrutiny that other major forces in culture need. It may in fact be true that we deserve more pats on the back than we get, both from our students and the public at large, but we cannot really know that unless we have examined ourselves closely. Like other people, however, academics postpone self-examination for the same reason that many of us postpone going to the dentist: Probing around in the soft nerve center of our assumptions and values sometimes hurts. Even when it does not hurt, it always makes us flinch.

Ethical criticism especially makes us flinch. What are the ethical implications, for example, of professionalism? If inefficiency, obfuscation, overspending, lack of accountability, lack of intelligibility, white-collar crime, political cover-ups, and theft of commercial ideas all suggest that nonacademic professionalism has its dangers, does it not stand to reason that academic professionalism must have its dangers too? Are academics' forays into jargon and double-speak any less objectionable than the same forays engaged in by politicians or other power brokers? Academic professionals consistently criticize their nonacademic counterparts, especially politicians and business persons, for exhibiting partisanship, prejudice, factionalism, self-indulgence, self-interestedness, and conflict of interest in their everyday dealings. But when and where do we seriously measure our own distance from or indulgence in these very same lapses? Our profession is Janus-faced: One countenance looks out on vistas of Socratic high-mindedness and selflessness, while the other looks out on vistas of power, competition, prestige, and money. Where and when do we seriously examine the tensions, conflicts, discrepancies, and hypocrisies potentially created by these two faces? For us to assume that our profession automatically lifts us above the pull of self-interestedness that other professions pull their practitioners down into is like putting on the emperor's new clothes. We cannot depend on others to heal the blindness of our self-infatuation, and we cannot forestall the necessity of examining ourselves by vague promises to be good. We need to institutionalize review and debate procedures for examining the compatibility of our everyday practices and our espoused principles: the way power is wielded, the pattern of promotions and salary raises, the commitment to affirmative action hiring, the depth of support for general education programs, and on and on. We cannot survive as institutions committed to the life of the mind without the self-knowledge that comes from self-examination.

We also inquire only slightly, if at all, into the ethics of teaching. All teaching is an invitation to one of the most intimate human experiences: the touching of minds. Whether the contact is jolting, reassuring, or revolting, it is almost always intimate. The teaching/learning act cannot occur unless the students make themselves vulnerable, unless they agree to lay open their pattern of thoughts and values and allow the teacher to suggest new arrangements. But the intimacy goes even deeper than this. While the teacher's knowledge and instruction suggest new ways of viewing ideas, events, and people, the *manner* of presentation suggests an entire ethos of how ideas, events, and people should be judged and evaluated. Teaching not only widens students' views of the ideas and judgments that exist in the world, but leads them to view some ideas as the best and some judgments as right. Even the teacher who tries to avoid explicit value judgments conveys them implicitly nevertheless. Doing so is an inherent part of teaching.

The question that academics must confront is not how to avoid influencing the values and character of their students, but how to make that inevitable influence nonmanipulative, noncoercive, and nondegrading. If our influentiality poses dangers, it also offers opportunities. Without it students could never develop very far beyond the limits that they live and think within when they come to us. Students under the influence of good teachers, like plants nourished with fertilizer, sometimes grow in exhilarating and powerful spurts. Any power this potent must be handled with great care, yet the ethical dimensions of this issue seldom receive treatment in professional journals or at conferences. One reason we avoid the issue is that ethical discussion in general has become more of a specialized province within philosophy, and less of a province with frontiers that touch the everyday areas and issues of life. A second reason is that academics have few good models of what the teaching/learning act is supposed to look like.

Are teachers like pitchers and students like batters, adversaries trying to get the best of each other? Are they like dancers, the teachers performing the leading steps which good students try to imitate perfectly? Are they like war buddies supporting each other in the trenches as they both fight a war against the system, bad luck, or life as a whole? Are they like coaches and trainers, priests and novitiates, or bosses and workers? Or are they like friends, not merely casual acquaintances and not merely people who fill up the blank spots in each other's social worlds the way Muzak fills up the blank spaces in our aural world, but real friends: persons who may not be equal in all of their abilities or acquirements, but who each desire that the other should grow into the best possible men or women. Our models will determine how we conduct ourselves.

The model that I see with increasing frequency, and the one

that worries me the most for what it masks, is the model of the teacher as a morally neutral conduit of morally neutral skills or objective knowledge: the teacher as depersonalized instructor. This model is highly charged with moral implications made seductively dangerous by its pretenses to objectivity. It masks the value judgments that go into the selection of materials and skills that are taught, as well as the value judgments that are an inescapable component of learning. It conveys the false impression that issues and problems can be solved on the basis of facts alone, and disguises that facts themselves, as philosophers of science have been telling us for the last twenty years, are always impregnated by theory and values. This model hinders teachers' attempts to deal with ethical issues by preventing those issues from even being seen. Hiding issues from sight is the worst danger of all, for the moral problems that usually hurt us the most are not necessarily the ones we cannot answer, but the ones we fail to see as questions. A few years ago, for example, it would never have occurred to most academics to ask what attitudes toward women as scholars, colleagues, and professionals a candidate for a dean should hold. By not even seeing this as an issue many injustices were done. We run the same risk of defaulting on moral issues in teaching when we think of — and evaluate — teaching solely in terms of disciplinary expertise or scholarly productivity.

The Influence of Mechanical Metaphors

A third obstacle to developing introductory courses that are vital to liberal education is a crippling subservience to mechanical metaphors. Educational talk has always and necessarily been sprinkled with metaphors and examples. Since the process of becoming educated is internal and invisible, metaphors and examples help make it concretely discussable. Throughout the history of educational talk the most congenial examples have been taken from human activities themselves, and the most congenial metaphors have been organic: metaphors that connote the growth, development, improvement, and functionality of the whole creature or being under discussion. When Socrates talks about education, for example, he typically uses metaphors about training animals or growing plants, or, most typically of all, talks about craftsmen who alone among all practitioners of the socially useful arts can not only say what they do but how they do it. They are the only ones who can teach as well as perform, and thus they often provide Socrates with his central examples about education. Throughout the centuries following Socrates, talk about education often traveled down narrower corridors in which various writers focused on what one needed to know, say, as a prince, as a priest, or as a philosopher, but the validity of talking about what human beings needed to know *as* human beings was never questioned. Nor was such talk ever completely abandoned; until recently it kept reappearing as the touchstone which made all other kinds of educational talk intelligible.

During the last 350 years, however, as the authority of classical philosophy and Christian morality has steadily waned, talk about education has consistently become less organic and more mechanical. It is not always recognized as being mechanical, even by those who use mechanical metaphors, but it is overwhelmingly so nevertheless. For example, the dominant metaphor in education today is *education as storage,* denoting the mechanical activity of stocking warehouses or piling things up on shelves. Most of the education that I received and most that I see around me has been grounded on the assumptions buried in this controlling metaphor. Its main implication is that the mind is so much physical space. The task of the school boards, boards of trustees, administrators, and teachers who accept this view is to fill up that intellectual space with retrievable educational material—portable property—while the student's task is to store it away in organized piles and categories available for periodic, mandatory display.

Departments and curriculum programs consistently subscribe to this view. As student travelers on diploma freeways pass through the service stations of various departments for fueling and fixing, the teachers toiling as station attendants view their job as filling each student's head with a specified number of cubic feet of departmental products before quickly shooting the students back onto the freeway. The crude, old-fashioned version of this metaphor is that the student's mind is either a warehouse or a filing cabinet. Those responsible for the student's education stuff as great a quantity of furniture or file folders into the space as they can, and hope it stays in place long enough for the student to demonstrate ownership. The modern, more sophisticated version of the metaphor is that the student's mind is a computer memory bank. Data labeled *input* are entered by the teacher; answers labeled *output* are occasionally called up for printout by the student. But regardless of how much better the computer version of the metaphor captures the electrical quickness of the mind's operations, all of these versions remain storage metaphors.

These storage metaphors have particularly negative effects on introductory courses. Among the reasons students consider these courses as hurdles to be overcome may be that they seem to be so full of inert matter: terms to learn by rote, objective tests to be machine-scored, and facts to be piled up. The faculty gravitate toward such preoccupations with facts because they afford shortcuts to teaching—or, more precisely, to processing—students on their way to more important learning in upper-division courses.

The storage metaphor oversimplifies the incredibly complex and essentially mysterious process of learning. It leads to a pedagogy that masks the ethical issues at the heart of the teaching/learning act, and it leads to modes of evaluation that have nothing to do with education's true end, "the end," as Sydney puts it, "of well doing and not of well knowing only." The storage metaphor says that the difference between an educated person and an uneducated person is always quantifiably measurable: One simply counts the student's bits of portable information. Most of what we call testing is designed precisely for this function. The idea that education is for well doing and not just for well knowing—the idea that our learning should somehow make the world a more congenial place for the flowering of the human spirit, the idea that knowledge is barren unless it gives birth to improved practices—is almost totally masked by this metaphor. We also need to recognize that stored pieces of knowledge, like photographic chemicals, have a limited shelf life: The ones that are not used every day eventually lose their potency or disintegrate altogether. Clearly, metaphors dominate our perceptions and experience. We cannot do without them, but in order to do with them they must be appropriate and they must be chosen with care.

A more appropriate metaphor for education than storage, for example, might be the eating of bread. Flour and yeast are separate substances, but when we take them in by eating we assimilate them so completely that flour and yeast become part of us: flesh of our flesh, bone of our bone. It is a wonderful and mysterious act, this taking in of lower-order substances, the not-us, and transmuting them through organic alchemy, into the us, into what we are. Our daily bread becomes not only the concrete matter of life, the eye-that-sees and the heart-that-pumps, but also becomes the more abstract energy of the soul-that-sees and the heart-that-feels. The staff of life that keeps the neurons firing, itself a process not fully understood, somehow becomes even more mysterious when it produces such acts as thoughts about Plato or speculations about the future.

Education should be like the eating of daily bread, an activity that nourishes the individual mind and the body politic the same way that flour and yeast nourish the body. Education should be alchemical transmutation of lower-order knowledge into higher-order wisdom. At the very least knowledge should be transmuted into the energy and quality of our response to experience. If education does not *inform* our lives by providing us with guiding principles, at the same time that it *informs* our minds by providing us with information, then the power of the word to become *logos* never materializes. As Matthew Arnold observed, the hunger that keeps us devouring knowledge is our hunger to answer the question, "How should I live?" Stored knowledge may help us answer discrete or mechanical kinds of questions—"What are Wordsworth's birth and death dates?"—but only knowledge that has been eaten and digested can help us answer the question, "How should I live?"

Conclusion

The implications of these ideas for introductory courses are both numerous and important. We need to get clear that all education should be based on liberal education (but not sacrificed to liberal education, an ambition that self-styled "pragmatists" frequently impute to defenders of liberal education). We must clarify our thinking about means and ends to reinvigorate discussion about the ethics of professionalism and teaching. We need to think critically about the influence of our controlling metaphors. If we approached education from these perspectives, we would do a great many things differently in education as a whole, but we would especially rethink and redesign our approaches to introductory courses.

First, we would teach less but teach better. That is, we would not force students to behave like frantic stock boys so busy throwing knowledge onto shelves that they have no time to examine it, think about it, discuss it, or evaluate it.

Second, we would either abandon objective and machine-scored tests, or at least complement them with essay tests. To give students the idea that the whole world of knowledge is divisible into little nuggets of gold or dross (true or false), or discrete categories from *a* to *e*—so unproblematic that even a machine can tell absolutely which categories are right and wrong—simply conveys a false view of knowledge and truth.

Third, we would systematically pursue appropriate connections between the material we teach and issues or problems in the outside world. Not all topics and courses lend themselves equally well to this task, of course, but many that do never have their larger implications underscored by teachers. Students will have more incentive to digest knowledge, not just store it, when its links to the world at large are not ignored.

Fourth, we would pursue the ethical implications of what we

teach, not with the aim of settling every issue of right and wrong for our students, but in order that they should learn how to raise and pursue ethical questions on their own.

Fifth, we would not pretend that facts comprise the only legitimate form of knowledge. While acknowledging that facts are important in arguments and often crucial as evidence both in scholarly pursuits and everyday dealings, we would nevertheless help students to see that most of the important questions they will face throughout their whole lives — whether to marry, whom to marry, how to raise children, what candidates to vote for, which college to select, whether to believe in God, what church to attend, what petitions to sign, and so on — can never be answered by an appeal to facts alone.

Sixth, we would force students to learn the art of discussion. Many students do not like class discussions these days, partly because they know that the content of discussions hardly ever turns up in recognizable form on objective tests. But if most of the important problems and questions that they face can be successfully answered only by developing opinions and not by merely checking out the facts, then students need to know how to refine and test their opinions in open discussion with others.

Seventh, we would teach students the art of critical thinking. In order to achieve intellectual autonomy, they must learn the art of using critical questions the way pearl divers use oyster knives, to discover the living matter and occasional jewels that lie beneath the surface formulations of issues.

Eighth, we would remember that education is supposed to help students develop wisdom, not just skills. Skills may make us more efficient, but only wisdom can keep us civilized. Skills may be put to destructive as well as constructive uses; only wisdom can help us tell the difference.

The most important thing that introductory courses do is to give students, including future teachers, a set of expectations about education as a whole. Those expectations will probably dominate the kind of commitment and energy that they devote to their whole four years of higher education, and, beyond that, to the standards they hold for the education of their children. Therefore, the character of education for society is indelibly colored by the character of introductory college courses. Clearly we who run our country's educational establishments need not only to take our responsibilities seriously, but to engage in unceasing and critical discussion about how we may fulfill them better.

Marshall W. Gregory is associate professor of English at Butler University in Indianapolis, Indiana, and director of the Lilly Endowment Post-Doctoral Teaching Awards Program.

The introductory course fulfills a number of goals for students and colleges, including recruitment and screening of majors, provision of prerequisite knowledge, explorations of learning, commitment to college, and cognitive development.

Challenges of the Introductory Course

Robert E. Dunham
Maryellen Gleason

The direction in which education starts a man will determine his future life.
Plato, *The Republic*, Book IV

Each year, 4,000 students are introduced to higher education at the University Park campus of the Pennsylvania State University. During their freshman year, they will select 750 different classes from among the 5,000 offered. However, freshman course selections tend to be more similar than they are different, due to university basic degree requirements. In fact, seventeen courses account for nearly 50 percent of all credit hours earned by freshmen. If the course total is raised to fifty-five, the share of credit hours accounted for climbs to 75 percent. These statistics suggest that there is a common and typical way in which students are introduced to higher education. Our goal is to describe that first encounter, explore the purposes of introductory courses, and assess how those purposes can best be accomplished.

The initial encounter with college can be made clearer by describing it in terms of a specific but hypothetical example, Fred Freshman.

K. I. Spear (Ed.). *Rejuvenating Introductory Courses*. New Directions for Teaching and Learning, no. 20. San Francisco: Jossey-Bass, December 1984.

When Fred arrives at Penn State, he has already declared a major: engineering. He and approximately 30 percent of his class arrive anxious to ride the giant technological wave. That Fred will in fact graduate in engineering and get the $24,000-a-year job that he anticipates is doubtful. Pitted against the rising College of Engineering entrance requirements, his Scholastic Aptitude Test scores and high school grade point average put him in a category of students very likely to change majors. But, for the moment, Fred has faith in himself and in the institution. He can make it; he is determined to work hard.

Because the last two years of the engineering curriculum is packed with the specialized courses of the major, Fred is advised to get his basic requirements out of the way first. It sounds as if those courses are not particularly important, but the suggestion comes from Fred's adviser, so he follows it, and enrolls in English, calculus, chemistry, anthropology, psychology, and engineering graphics.

With new notebook and sharp pencils in hand, Fred heads off to begin his college career. The English class has twenty-four students, none of whom Fred has met before. His instructor, like 65 percent of the instructors who teach English 15, is a graduate teaching assistant. She has completed one year of course work toward her master's degree, she is twenty-four years old, and she has never taught a course. Like Fred, she is determined to do a good job. She is apprehensive but enthusiastic. During the next fifteen weeks, Fred writes seven papers for the course. The experience is designed to provide him with the instruction and practice necessary to write acceptable, expository prose.

In calculus, the atmosphere is not quite so intimate. Three hundred and fifty students, none of whom Fred has met before, convene in a large lecture hall. The course meets there three days a week to hear formal lecture presentations covering the basic principles of calculus and geometry. Fred is worried about what he will do if he needs help in the course, but he is somewhat relieved when he learns that a once-a-week recitation session is part of the course. On that day, twenty to thirty students meet with a graduate student, who responds to individual questions. Chemistry 12 is organized similarly. Between three hundred and fifty and four hundred students attend a lecture three days a week, and groups of twenty-five to thirty students meet two days a week under the tutelage of a recitation instructor — a graduate student.

Psychology 2 is another large class about the same size as the math and chemistry classes, but it lacks the recitation opportunities. The instructor — a tenured associate professor — and his assistant — a graduate student — make themselves available for a total of eight hours a week to discuss course-related issues. Grades for this course are determined by scores on four fifty-point multiple-choice tests and a final. The person sitting next to Fred tells him that copies of previous exams are "around."

The Purposes of Introductory Courses

Fred's courses show the different purposes that introductory courses can serve. Courses such as engineering graphics represent a student's first encounter with a field. Although Fred knows enough about engineering to claim it for a major, he knows virtually nothing about the experimental methods of measurement and graphic expressions that comprise the content of the course. This is not the case in chemistry and English. Fred took both in high school. At the college level, he is being introduced to higher and more complex levels. The English course serves another purpose as well: to enhance the development of writing skills useful now and in the future. Chemistry is another dual-purpose course. Not only does Fred find out more about a field, but the content of the course provides him with a knowledge base that subsequent, more specialized courses will require him to apply. Still another purpose can be identified in the anthropology course. The area is new to Fred—not something of interest. Course content is not prerequisite. Anthropology illustrates how an introductory course can be liberalizing—an encounter with new experiences that broadens intellectual vistas.

The example of Fred illustrates the present situation, but is the present situation the ideal? Is that what introductory encounters should be like? That question can best be answered by exploring both the actual and the possible purposes of introductory courses.

Introduction to Academic Areas. Introductory courses encourage encounters with new ideas and information. In some instances, students are being introduced to total strangers, that is, to areas in which they have no previous experience. In others they are being asked to meet friends of friends, that is, academic areas related to others they know. In still other instances, subjects to which they have already been introduced appear in different contexts. Previous encounters were brief and superficial, now the associations will be longer and more intimate.

Introductions between persons provide a useful model for the goals and objectives of introductions to content areas. Introductions are performed by persons who know the individuals being introduced. Sometimes, the two have just met; sometimes they have been lifelong companions. In both instances, what the person making the introduction can say about the other is a function of familiarity. Also, because introductions are brief, they focus on essentials — names, occupations, accomplishments — the obvious means of identifying a person. The ability to do that well depends on prior knowledge not just of one but of both individuals. A good introduction tells one something about the other that permits a sense of identification and makes subsequent interactions a comfortable possibility. Finally, impressions are formed during first meetings that affect subsequent encounters. In our society, the need to make good first impressions is heavily emphasized.

So, when the purpose is to introduce a student to a field about which he or she is relatively uninformed, the quality of the introduction depends greatly on instructors' knowledge of their disciplines and of their students. A skillful academic introduction leaves the student both able and willing to continue the association. Finally, the beginning course ought to be impressive, so that it fosters favorable conclusions about the content area and higher education.

Recruitment of Majors. In Fred's situation, the prognosis for change of major is extremely high, but that is true of college students generally. Fifty percent of undergraduates change their major at least once, and there is evidence at Penn State that about 80 percent seriously consider the possibility. In days of declining enrollment, the recruitment function of introductory courses ought to be taken seriously.

What factors influence the choice of major? Certainly, future employment possibilities play a significant role in the student's decision making, but that is not the only factor. Students opt for academic areas that they like, which generally means that they do well in the courses and that they are impressed with their instructors. However, recruitment interests are not well served by easy courses that aim only to please. Instructors should be good professional role models. In a typology of teachers, Mann and others (1970) explain the point this way: Students see professors as members of a community of scholars. As such, they illustrate the values, assumptions, and style of intellectual life that characterize the discipline. From introductory courses students conclude what it is like to be a historian, a physicist, a political scientist, or a linguist. More important, they ask the question, Is this what I want to be like?

It is equally important for the faculty of a department to recruit students who are suitable to major in the field. Introductory courses can serve an important gatekeeping function. They permit members of an academic area to screen prospective majors. Even though some fields badly need to increase their enrollments, their ultimate interests will not be served by accepting all students. So, the initial encounter provides an early opportunity to assess suitability.

Provision of Prerequisite Knowledge. Introductory classes often initiate a series or sequence of courses. At Penn State, Math 140 is followed by Math 141, Physics 201 by Physics 202. The second, third, or fourth course in a sequence assumes familiarity with a common content foundation. To the extent that a foundation is largely responsible for the structural stability of anything built upon it, the beginning course occupies a fundamental position. In addition, if students come to an introductory course poorly prepared, ill equipped to lay the foundation, or both, the instructional challenge increases proportionately.

Exploration of Learning. Students entering college have much experience in learning, but higher education shifts the focus from learning as means to learning as end. Combining diverse curricular components into a set of basic degree requirements has a synergistic effect. The experience provides skills for lifelong learning and develops the capacity to integrate learning with past and present experiences. Arons (1978, p. 113) makes the point this way: "The time is long past that we can teach our students all the things they must know. It is hardly an original assertion that the only viable and realistic function of higher education is to put students on their own intellectual feet: to give them conceptual starting points and an awareness of what it means to learn and understand something."

Introductory courses can make special contributions to the accomplishment of these learning objectives in three ways. First, the introduction of students to unfamiliar content areas has the potential to expand learning skills. Simply stated, different academic areas approach problem solving in different ways. Mathematical and psychological solutions look different. The methodology of the detached, objective, scientist examining isolated variables in a sterile environment must be adapted if it is to explain behavior in the messy, unpredictable climate of human relations. So, students taking a variety of courses begin to discover that many roads are traveled in quest of the unknown, and in the experience they learn a lot about learning.

The goal also is to use all college courses, but introductory courses especially, to further essential cognitive development: specifically, to teach students how to think. The aim is noble, and academicians appropriately offer their allegiance. Ask instructors the question, Five years after taking your course, what is it you want students to remember? and they rarely answer with descriptions of content. Very often, they list analytical, critical, and creative thinking abilities. Yet, the instructional challenge of the task is often overlooked. It is almost as if educational practitioners believe the results occur automatically — as if the presence of academic content is enough to cause the desired cognitive outcomes to rub off on students' minds. Disturbing survey results reported by Gaff (1978) pinpoint a potential problem: Although 78 percent of an almost 1,700 faculty sample said they attached much or great importance to learning to critically analyze ideas, only 27 percent of an almost 3,500 students sample said that a majority of their class time was spent on such activities. Although it is quite easy to describe the cognitive experience with erudition, it may in fact be very difficult to translate the desired outcome into concrete teaching practices.

Finally, introductory survey courses have the potential to enhance learning objectives by virtue of the sweeping content areas covered. They are less confined to specifics and more open to generalizations. As such, they can serve the integrative and synthetic functions that make it possible to combine and correlate past and present experience. They can make the pieces of knowledge fit together and thereby broaden student perspectives.

Advancing Student Development. Whether one subscribes to Piaget, Perry, or any of a host of other developmental psychologists, the conclusion is the same. Students change in college, and courses should be designed to further the cognitive, moral, ethical, and esthetic maturation process. However, the conclusion should not be construed to imply that development occurs automatically. Kohlberg and Mayer (1978, p. 163) dispel that myth by pointing out "that a concept of stages as 'natural' does not mean that they are inevitable; many individuals fail to attain the higher stages of logical and moral reasoning." In other words, this aim is accomplished only if the instructor is highly knowledgeable about young adult development and individual student progress.

Increasing the Commitment to College. Stated explicitly, the purpose to be fulfilled is this: At Penn State (and figures for other institutions are similar), 45 percent of the total attrition in a given class occurs by the beginning of the second year. The critical time for decisions to stay or leave is the freshman year, and the research on retention confirms the suspicion that students are more likely to stay than leave if they are having positive experiences in courses and with instructors. Moreover, the most common course and instructor experiences of first-year students are those provided by introductory courses. In spite of current economic exigencies, the concern is as altruistic as it is financial, The decision for or against a college education has implications that extend far beyond its effect on a given institution. The student is really making a decision about the subsequent quality of life.

Accomplishing the Purposes of Introductory Courses

The preceding discussion makes it clear that the aims and objectives for students' first encounters with higher education just stated are not unrealistic. Despite economic pressures and the general move toward consumerism and accountability, the purposes ought to be the actual outcomes of a college education. That leads quite logically to the question of how: How are purposes like these best accomplished within our institutions? The answer involves the faculty who teach the courses, the students who take the courses, and the climates in which the instruction occurs.

Faculty. Four faculty characteristics influence the identified purposes. First, faculty need to be content-competent. This means that they must know what and how knowledge foundations are laid. Content competence also assumes the ability to construct a bird's-eye view of a field that maintains its perspective. The introductory course should condense and distill the discipline so that, even from a distance, the student sees the lay of the land and where this track lies in relation to others. Finally, content competence demands the ability to communicate explicitly to students how the discipline looks for answers, why the methodology works, and what makes the approach unique. In other words, content competence is more than facile footwork with the details of a field.

Faculty who teach introductory courses also need to be representative role models. They should typify scholars in the academic area. And, if this attribute is to serve recruitment, introductory courses must be taught with enthusiasm—an obvious interest, even an excitement about the field.

Teachers of introductory courses must be knowledgeable about students. Here, the necessary knowledge derives in part from experience that enables the instructor to know (not absolutely but probably) how students will respond to course material, what causes them difficulty, and what interests, challenges, motivates, and bores them. However, knowledge about students should be derived from more than interaction between students and course content. It should include an understanding of developmental issues—the process of maturation in young adults and the reflection of this understanding in systematic efforts to develop curricular components and class experiences that expedite development. And, it is broader in the sense of understanding students' interests so that communication with them can cross generation gaps and to make curricular content appropriate to the world in which they live.

Finally, persons who teach introductory courses must be pedagogically perceptive. The assertion here concerns pedagogical prowess. It means being aware of the impact of various instructional strategies and being able to apply that awareness. Teaching style is fixed in that it represents the individual and flexible in that it responds to the reality of a given classroom situation. The pulse of the class is monitored: Learning activities and experiences are dynamic responses the the rhythm of the class. The situation requires the acumen of an experienced and effective teacher.

Students. And, how do students help to accomplish the aims of introductory courses? Here, the institution has fewer points of control. Education is not something that is done to someone. Learning is not a spectator sport. No amount of adjustments will produce the aims desired of introductory courses if students do not assume their responsibility in the educational encounter. However, the institution does have the responsibility to apprise them of their accountability. Instructors must make the students aware that they have a role in accomplishing the goals of introductory courses, and saying it is never enough. Courses must be designed and instruction delivered in ways that prevent students from being passive.

Climates. If the goals of introductory courses are to be accomplished, the climates in which the learning occurs need to be intimate, interactive, and investigative. Climates need to be intimate, with faculty recognizing and responding to individuals. There is no magic class size at which this automatically occurs. Knapp (1976) characterizes a "destudentized" classroom as a place where there is no chance for informal student feedback or questions; a conviction that students really do not want to learn; an overemphasis on grades, which become the highest reward that an instructor can give to students; a voice of authority that is to be more trusted and valued than independent judgment; and an attempt to control student behavior by punitive actions. The climate of a destudentized classroom is not a function of size and can occur in a seminar or large lecture.

Climates conducive to the achievement of introductory course objectives also need to be interactive — characterized by an exchange of ideas, a sense of shared involvement, and reciprocity. Again, achievement of the goal is not necessarily a function of class size. Certainly, the challenge to involve students increases with class size, but an atmosphere in which ideas intermingle can be created by a variety of strategies; it is not exclusively a function of the ability to ask and answer student questions.

Finally, atmospheres in which the purposes of introductory

courses are accomplished need to be investigative — perhaps *exploratory* is a better word. Such classrooms need to convey a sense of discovery, the spirit of adventure. The energy, excitement, and challenge that accompany any expedition to parts unknown ought to characterize these learning environments. The expedition analogy is apt, because there is risk. Students need to learn in climates that encourage them to take chances, but they also need the support of someone experienced enough to know both the dangers and the precautions that the situation demands. Hill (1980, p. 48) develops other aspects of the analogy: "The guide recognizes that success. . . depends upon the close coooperation, active participation of each member of the group. He has crossed the terrain before and is familiar with the landmarks, but each trip is new and generates its own anxiety and excitement."

Reconciling the Real with the Ideal

The purposes identified for introductory courses are not pie in the sky, but the ways they are best accomplished may appear to be, especially when they are juxtaposed with the freshman experience described at the beginning of this chapter. Fred is not real, but the courses described are. Although Fred's experience is fabricated, it represents a first encounter with higher education that is common at Penn State. In this section, we reconcile the reality of the experience with the ideal of accomplishing the aims.

The ideal could be accomplished if the reality were changed. This would mean significant reductions in class size and substantial re-allocation of funds to prepare faculty for teaching introductory courses. The possibility of its occurring at a large, research-oriented institution or even at a small private university is slim. Introductory courses have low priority among faculty and tempt administrators to stretch budgets by keeping classes large and using comparatively cheaper graduate student staff. So, it seems unlikely that Fred and twenty other freshmen will take Chemistry 12 from a full professor with two teaching awards and three research fellowships to her credit. With radical change ruled out, consider some realistic possibilities for improving introductory courses in terms of faculty, students, and climates.

Faculty. Faculty can be better equipped to accomplish the aims of introductory courses. In some respects, the solution is simple — provide faculty with information and encourage them to interact. How often do instructors within and across disciplines sit down and discuss the purposes of introductory courses or the stages of student maturation? They could profitably do so — reminding themselves and those new among them precisely what they intend to accomplish and with whom.

With the objectives clearly in mind, the next question is how, not who but how. The distinction is important. The question how generates answers that describe instructional strategies, the ways and means by which one might introduce academic areas, recruit majors, advance student development, and increase students' commitment to college. To ask who is to restrict the discussion to groups and individuals. Given the reality of the educational world in which introductory courses are taught today, teaching assistants, untenured professors, and atypical academicians are usually responsible for introductory courses. With answers to the question how there is at least the possibility of providing faculty members with potentially useful information.

The good news from decades of research on instruction is that many of the hows are known or are at least to the place of being pretty good possibilities. For example, if the aim is to help students expand their repertoire of learning skills, the research of Kolb (1976), Dunn and Dunn (1978), Riechmann and Grasha (1974), and others on learning styles presents a fairly clear picture of how general categories of students go about the learning task. Instructional strategies can be developed to enhance an individual's style or to encourage the individual to explore another.

If the goal is to increase pedagogical prowess so that instructors become better able to create memorable impressions, manage instructional strategies that further cognitive development, or present more content to less-prepared students efficiently, then the hows determined by research for faculty and instructional development can be applied. To cite a few examples, teaching evaluations can include a feedback mechanism to improve instruction. Videotaped samples of teaching can be analyzed by individual instructors, experts, or both to provide a clear assessment of instructional impact. Characteristics frequently identified as components of effective instruction have been isolated, and they can be described behaviorally, so that teaching staff can talk with some precision about what effective instructors do and about how they might incorporate those features into their own teaching style.

The list could go on, but the point should be clear. Equipping faculty to teach introductory courses is not only possible but a real and legitimate part of the solution. The claim holds true even if the instructor is an inexperienced teaching assistant. The hard questions about the preparedness of teaching assistants to teach and about their representativeness as role models remain, but issues of preparedness and representativeness are not restricted to them. Moreover, most universities are far more systematic and thorough in providing training for teaching assistants than they are for faculty at large. This is not to say that universities are systematic and thorough in preparing teaching assistants to teach introductory courses but to underscore that at most institutions the mechanisms for additional training already exist. Finally, although the use of teaching assistants in introductory courses poses problems, it also has some unique and important advantages. Pickering (1983, p. 56) identifies several worth noting: "They are young, energetic, and enthusiastic. . . teaching is a new experience for them; they haven't yet had time to become bored with the material or impatient at constantly answering the same question."

To summarize, the extent to which the purposes of the introductory course are accomplished rests to a large degree on the shoulders of the instructors who teach them. Institutions should encourage an energetic shouldering of that responsibility by providing instructors with appropriate information and opportunities to prepare.

Students. There are two problems with students that diminish their contribution to the goals of introductory courses. In both cases, instructors and institutions can effect changes. First, students are not yet aware that introductory courses exist for reasons other than to present content. Second, they do not see any coherence or correlation among the courses that constitute the basic degree requirements. For them, the pieces of information presented by diverse disciplines stand or fall on their own. Students do not see the importance of such courses, and the advice that Fred received to get them out of the way reinforces this conclusion.

The answer lies not in fixing blame. Many persons, policies, attitudes, and ideas have contributed. The solution requires an affirmation of what education is all about and a new tack with instructional strategies. This is what a Penn State professor did recently: The course began as usual with the distribution of the syllabus and discussion of its contents, including a list of course goals. The second day of class, the instructor began by discussing an itemized list of course objectives presented on an overhead transparency. Students listened politely but waited until the "real" lecture started before taking notes. Two weeks into the course, the instructor asked students to take five minutes to prepare a list of the course goals. The thirty-two lists submitted contained forty-five different goals—forty more than the syllabus listed. Less than 20 percent of the class was able to describe one of the identified goals correctly. The instructor discussed the results with students, and they jointly agreed that every content segment, learning activity, out-of-class assignment, and in-class discussion would thereafter be related explicitly to at least one of the goals, so that everyone would understand what the activity aimed to accomplish.

Another problem relates to students' passivity — their frequent obvious lack of involvement in the learning process. Gross (1980) attributes the problem to competition from the entertainment world. The images provided by television, movies, and video are captivating, professional, and technically sophisticated, and they are designed to be taken in with nothing given back. While Gross does not despair of the less than polished professorial performance, he reminds us (p. 36) that the classroom has one compelling advantage, because the "teacher is human, responding to the humanity of the students before him, adjusting and adapting, making connections. And therein lies the advantage. . . . Great teaching is the electric current of two minds enlightening one another."

Climates. To accomplish the aims of introductory courses successfully, instructional environments need to be intimate, interactive, and investigative. The classrooms of Fred's freshman experience cannot be so characterized. Obviously, class size creates a problem, but the dominant instructional strategies only make it worse. In the classroom, communication goes in one direction: The instructor talks. Research by Smith (1977) shows that even in smaller classes where there was an opportunity for interaction, instructors questioned students only 2.6 percent of the time, and students participated 14.2 percent of the time. That educational environments are neither intimate nor interactive is easy to document. Are they investigative? Is there a sense of exploration, discovery, adventure? The answer is: not usually. In most classrooms, the pace is pedantic. Students trudge into class, professors plod through lecture notes, and both leave weary and wondering why. There is very little of Hill's (1980, p. 48) notion of "expeditions of shared responsibility into the most exciting and least understood terrain on earth — the mind itself."

Although class size is not likely to change, classroom climates can be altered. Their cold impersonality can be cracked. And, the changes desired can often result from attention to small details. In large lecture settings, the instructor can arrive early and circulate around the room talking to students. The professor can stand at the door handing out papers or collecting exams. The instructor treats the large space as though it were very small, being equally at ease behind the podium, before the front row, up the middle aisle, or at the side chalkboard. One Penn State instructor solves the names dilemma by sharing the responsibility with students: If they want to be known, they must help by introducing themselves, by participating in class, by dropping in at the office, and by greeting him when they see him. In his large chemistry class, he uses the names he knows to make the atmosphere more personal.

The climate can become more interactive when the instructor develops strategies of interaction with students and increases the opportunities for them to exchange with each other. Too often, learning environments and classrooms are considered one and the same. In fact, much can and should be accomplished outside the classroom, thus encouraging and assisting students to be more responsible for their own learning.

Within the classroom, climates can be made interactive by using closed questioning strategies, which require short answers and which can be moved through quickly. Rhetorical questions can be used in ways that provoke thought. Students' contributions can always be recognized, even if only by phrases like *students often ask me* or *a student once made the observation that.*

Climates in classes can also become more investigatory. The solution is not so simple here, but the place to begin could be with an affirmation of student ability. One of the unfortunate consequences of our national concern with student deficiencies has been a general depreciation of their assets. Students are not without redeeming features, and faculty would do well to remind themselves of the actual and potential contributions of students to our institutional and individual enrichment. Perhaps if we appreciated students more at the onset of their college careers, it would be easier to invite them to explore the light and dark areas of our understanding.

Introductory courses are an important part of the educational experience. What Plato says is true: Education determines future directions. In the case of introductory courses, these directions must become clearer and more complete than they have been in the past.

References

Arons, A. B. "Teaching Science." In S. M. Cahn (Ed.), *Scholars Who Teach.* Chicago: Nelson-Hall, 1978.

Dunn, R., and Dunn, K. *Teaching Students Through Their Individual Learning Styles.* Reston, Va.: Reston, 1978.

Gaff, J. G. "Overcoming Faculty Resistance." In J. G. Gaff (Ed.), *Institutional Renewal Through the Improvement of Teaching.* New Directions for Higher Education, no. 24. San Francisco: Jossey-Bass, 1978.

Gross, T. L. "Inside Room 307." *Change,* 1980, *12* (1), 32–38.

Hill, N. K. "Scaling the Heights: The Teacher as Mountaineer." *Chronicle of Higher Education,* June 16, 1980, p. 48.

Knapp, M. L. "Communicating with Students." *Improving College and University Teaching,* 1976, *25* (3), 167–168.

Kohlberg, L., and Mayer, R. "Development as the Aim of Education." *Harvard Educational Review,* 1978, 242, 123–170.

Kolb, D. *Learning Style Inventory: Technical Manual.* Boston: McBer, 1976.

52

Mann, R. D., and others. *The College Classroom: Conflict, Change, and Learning.* New York: Wiley, 1970.

Pickering, M. "Should Teaching Assistants Be Asked to Play the Part of Socrates?" *Chronicle of Higher Education,* June 29, 1983, p. 56.

Riechmann, S., and Grasha, T. "A Rational Approach to Developing and Assessing the Construct Validity of a Student Learning Style Scales Instrument." *Journal of Psychology,* 1974, *87,* 213–233.

Smith, D. G. "College Classroom Interactions in Critical Thinking." *Journal of Educational Psychology,* 1977, *69* (2), 180–190.

Robert E. Dunham is professor of speech communication and vice-president for academic services at Pennsylvania State University, University Park, Pennsylvania.

Maryellen Gleason is head of the instructional development program at Pennsylvania State University.

*Many social and intellectual forces focus introductory courses
not on the process of inquiry but on its products.*

Knowledge, Mind, and Facts

Robert N. McCauley

In *The Great Conversation* Robert Maynard Hutchins (1952) argues that
the purpose of education is to develop a good mind, which means improving our analytical, critical, and imaginative powers while cultivating the moral and intellectual virtues. The problem with most courses
in general and with most introductory courses in particular is that they
fail on both counts. They fail to develop good minds, because too often
we simply forget that that is what they should do. Instead, we are usually satisfied if they are simply about history or about biology or about
some other discipline. In each of these areas, we have the facts, and we
are anxious to dispense them. In our enthusiasm to do just that, we
tend to overlook the fragmented picture of education and knowledge
that is implicitly presented in higher education. In contrast to that picture, which I will discuss at some length in this chapter, I suggest that
education resides not in the collection and distribution of the products
of our inquiries but rather in the process of inquiring.

Empiricism and Facts

The focus on intellectual products instead of their production
coheres with a host of modern social (McCauley, 1982) and intellectual
prejudices. Not the least of the latter is our empiricist predilection for
atomistic accounts of cognitive phenomena. For nearly 300 years,

K. I. Spear (Ed.). *Rejuvenating Introductory Courses.* New Directions for Teaching
and Learning, no. 20. San Francisco: Jossey-Bass, December 1984.

54

empiricism has remained faithful to Locke's general vision of the genesis and structure of knowledge as increasingly complex combinations of simple ideas occasioned by elementary features of sense experience. On this account, most of our knowledge is the result of various mental operations on these epistemic building blocks. This position can quickly reduce the development of good minds to the distribution and collection of bits of information.

Mind as Container. A preoccupation with education as the acquisition of bits of knowledge not surprisingly impoverishes our view of the mind. On this account, the mind is like a box. We pour the products of our inquiries into it, and we periodically sample its contents in order to test its integrity as a container. This view is inadequate in at least two crucial respects. If our minds are containers, they are porous at best. What we forget in a lifetime dwarfs what we remember. If nonporousness is the true mark of a good mind, then almost no one has had a good mind. This failure has not seriously undermined our ability to get on in the world, because we have developed many tools, ranging from notes to computer memory, that do such work in our stead. However, we are not particularly distraught about this situation. Because we have developed such powerful mnemonic aids, the simple storing of knowledge has now become one of our more mundane intellectual accomplishments. The second reason why the view of the mind as container is impoverished is that it completely ignores the intellectual powers that we have not learned to duplicate mechanically—judgment, insight, imagination, and reason (Rorty, 1982). These capacities atrophy when education requires no more of a human being than the passive storage of facts.

This product orientation suggests a view of education that often seems plausible, because it touches the truth here and there. Good minds usually know a lot of things. Poor minds usually do not. But, to yield to the temptation of defining educated minds as boxes of stored information is to encourage both arrogance and laziness. On this view, we are content to instruct (from a Latin root meaning to pile upon) rather than to educate (from a Latin root meaning to lead or draw out), because it is both easier to do and easier to certify. In one sense, piling knowledge on students places the burden on them. It absolves us if they fail. Their minds leak. If, on this view, we fail, that is, if what we dispense proves to be less than the full truth, then the extent of our culpability is equally ridiculous. If education is primarily the dispensation of facts, then we had better be positive about what we are dispensing. In any event, this view of teaching and learning ignores a crucial feature of intellectual growth, namely, the direct interaction of human minds.

Passing out the facts is simply not enough. Learners must grapple with one another by grappling with one another's ideas. A picture of education that shows more experienced learners leading less experienced learners portrays an evenhanded activity in which every participant has some measure of responsibility for fruitful interchange.

Too often, we are happy to pile the things we know on our students, because our intellectual accumulations and the efforts that we expend to retain them impress us so. We lack both Socratic humility and initiative. We have confused the energy required for the mnemonic maintenance of an idea with the energy that it releases during intellectual fission. We are so busy collecting, storing, and measuring knowledge that we overlook the fact that these activities are only one aspect of cultivating a good mind. It is by no means sufficient.

An Alleged Scientific Connection. Empiricist epistemology has gained credence beyond its intrinsic merits from its association with the successes of empirical science. However, careful scrutiny of this allegedly privileged association over the past two decades in the philosophy of science finds it generally wanting. It is particularly ironic, then, that the scientific community has so often fallen prey, especially in introductory courses, to the product-oriented instructional model implicit in modern empiricism. Kuhn (1970) describes this phenomenon; Thomas (1981), Eiseley (1978), and others have deplored it. The explanatory and predictive successes of scientific pronouncement in conjunction with their frequent mathematical complexity lend them a gravity that is guaranteed to command obeisance from novices but also, as Eiseley (1978) puts it, to blunt their wonder. If students remain generally unacquainted with the tremendous controversies that lie behind most scientific facts, the towering accomplishments of science will simply overwhelm them. Overwhelmed minds are immobilized minds, unlikely to consider the possibility that things might not be as we have all been told. (The humanities provoke less intense epistemic allegiance. This is because their products are less determinant. Consequently, the inadequacies of instruction focused predominantly on the products of inquiry are even more obvious in humanities courses.)

Kuhn's (1970) account of the histories of the sciences construes them as series of extended periods of authoritarian calm (what Kuhn calls *normal science*) punctuated by periodic revolutionary upheavals. With surprising frequency, outsiders have provoked these revolutions. Examples include Dalton in chemistry, Crick in genetics, and Einstein in physics. In some of the most important episodes, it is clear that normal science, that is, standard education and research in a particular field, has not been the primary engine of discovery.

56

Scientific progress does not depend essentially on narrow specialization or mastery of all the facts. Popper (1972) offers principled arguments against the view that progress in science is ever a function of either the accumulation or the manipulation of facts. All facts are theory-laden, because it is only in the larger framework of theory that facts become intelligible. A simple illustration may help. At the turn of the seventeenth century, the dawning of each new day was an undisputed fact. The quarrel was not over that fact but rather over what was to be made of it. The controversial question was whether the diurnal pattern was a function of the earth's or the sun's motion. Sometimes, the role of theory is quite obvious in our interpretation of the facts — for example, in the case of the path that a particle takes through a bubble chamber, an apparatus whose function is inscrutable when divorced from our theories of subatomic physics. In our everyday dealings with the world, however, we are more likely to forget the implicit theoretical commitments underlying common sense. Modern common sense, for example, is thoroughly Copernican on a number of counts. It has not always been so. Sometimes, our implicit commonsense theories are demonstrably flawed. Science surpassed much of our persisting mechanical common sense in the late Middle Ages. Today, subjects can fail to solve many extremely simply mechanical problems because they either do not have the concept of inertia or they choose to ignore it (McCloskey, 1983).

The point is that the facts are always changing, even in science, that preeminent knowledge-seeking activity. They change because theoretical innovations offer new ways of construing the world and therefore new accounts of the phenomena in question. I do not deny that there may be a great deal of continuity between one successful theory and another, but I want to emphasize the importance of our imaginative accomplishments in science and the alterations they inspire in what we take to be the facts.

The Insufficiency of Facts

Mastery of Facts. If undergraduate education in general and introductory courses in particular primarily emphasize the mastery of facts, the products of our inquiries, then they fail to enhance many faculties essential both to the cultivation of good minds and to the progress of those inquiries. In addition, they incur the very practical risk of dispensing truths that are out of date. Interesting problems require insight, but insight almost never issues from the mere collection of knowledge. Instead, it guides our decisions about what knowledge to collect.

Thus, the talk about mastery of facts is misleading. If students do not appreciate the historical, polemical, and conceptual contexts from which facts emerge, it is likely that the facts will dominate the students. Facts dominate when we do not know how to use them. We can only master facts when we have made the systems of ideas that inform them our own. It is through novel ideas and novel connections of ideas that we discover new facts and new ways of using the old ones. Mastery of facts is a consequence of disciplined inquiry, not its goal. Such mastery is unattainable for its own sake.

Beyond Facts. It is precisely in the extent to which theories go beyond facts that they become empirically interesting. The facts are about how the world is (or is alleged to be). The growth of knowledge results from the success of theoretical conjectures, which not only reveal new facts but contradict some of the old ones. The facts are necessary, but as props on the stage, not as actors. The drama of inquiry (and inquiry *is* dramatic) is necessarily a result of human interchange and the confrontation of our schemes for dealing with the world. The roles demand talents that only human beings can supply. The dramas that we live require active human minds, not passive ones. It is no coincidence that Socratic inquiry takes the form of dialogue and conversation. These activities involve human beings in attacking problems by attempting to make something of the facts, not merely by reciting them.

We must step beyond facts to discover the truths that give them meaning. Discoveries are the result of a laborious ongoing process of assessing how our most carefully formulated conjectures withstand the critical onslaughts of others. The growth of knowledge, both corporately and individually, requires the systematic development of four interlocking powers: first, the imagination to formulate new conjectures; second, the analytical ability to discover their structure, their relation to the evidence, and the problem-solving strategies that motivate them; third, the judgment to recognize and devise telling criticisms; and fourth, the skill to communicate our ideas accurately to fellow inquirers.

Mixed Messages

The exercise of these capacities is crucial to the progress of our inquiries and to the development of good minds. Such exercise should be the central focus of undergraduate education in general and of introductory courses in particular. Unfortunately, both undergraduate education and introductory courses often have other priorities. We have convinced ourselves that we can efficiently dispense, systematically present, technologically manipulate, safely store, exactly measure, and readily divide knowledge into discrete domains. Our declarations in support of liberal education notwithstanding, many dimensions of introductory courses disclose how much faith we put into this account of education as essentially the distribution and collection of facts.

The Setting. The notion that any long-term educational experience for introductory students can occur exclusively in a lecture hall indicates inadequate concern for the cultivation of good minds. The seating design directs students' attention to a single point in the room, from whence the truth shall issue. Such rooms have been designed for the pronouncements of experts, not for the conversations of learners. They discourage students from looking at one another, let alone learning from one another. In fact, they pressure professors to deliver lectures, because they clearly signal who is to do all the talking. This produces the all too familiar scenes of students so preoccupied with their notebooks (or so confident in their tape recorders) that they miss the power of the ideas that they preserve. Students have little or no opportunity to test their ideas by returning them to us. To compensate, schools sometimes schedule discussion sessions. However, the fact that these sessions are the responsibility of graduate assistants whenever possible clearly indicates how important the institutions hold them to be. Similarly, the fact that rigidly hierarchical departments often assign introductory courses to their most junior members indicates the esteem in which these courses are held.

The fact that so many introductory courses take place in such contexts has curricular implications as well. In philosophy, the expanding emphasis on symbolic logic in introductory logic classes is, at least in part, a function of the fact that the courses are increasingly taught in these large lecture settings. Arguments in natural language lack the rigor of formal systems. Hence, they do not submit to the tailoring that straightforward lecturing requires. Consequently, it is quite tempting to restrict or even eliminate this segment from the course. Of course, the problem is that arguments in natural language are the kind we all make.

Parallel phenomena in other fields have created an additional problem that concerns about enrollment only exacerbate. Approaching introductory courses as opportunities to recruit for particular disciplines inevitably misses the mark. Recent notions that most late adolescents either could or should know what field on which to focus or what occupation to pursue are preposterous. (This is not a necessary truth. It is an irony that excessive emphasis on career education defeats itself. If our system of education was in fact generally committed to the development of good minds, students might be ready as new undergraduates to make such decisions in large numbers. However, encouraging students to make these choices prematurely tends only to perpetuate intellectual blight.)

Written Work. The format of written assignments in general and of examinations in particular also provides clues about our educational priorities. If written assignments focus overwhelmingly on the sort of work susceptible to machine grading, then we communicate quite effectively (albeit unconsciously) our expectations about the extent of their educational experiences. Even the most cleverly designed objective tests fail to examine the most crucial skill in the process of inquiry, namely, our ability to present and defend our positions in an economical, accurate, and clear verbal form. Such tests elicit only the products of our inquiries, not the processes by which we reach them. They look only at our conclusions. They ignore the reasons that we would cite to support them. People can arrive at the same conclusion for all sorts of reasons. It is important to know whether students come to their conclusions by sound reasoning, faulty reasoning, or random guessing.

The distinction between participating in this process and describing it (presumably after the fact) is arbitrary on a number of counts. The describing is the last and most important step in the process by which we reach the conclusions that we claim as our own. It is only when we must display our thinking to others for their critical inspection that we get our best view of how the products of that process stack up. Assignments that neglect this final step demonstrate our willingness to settle for half-baked ideas. They also communicate to students that it is only the products that matter, not also the logical rigor, strategic efficiency, and moral acceptability of their methods.

Turf. Reverent respect for disciplinary boundaries is another sure sign of where we put our faith. This suggests to students that we regard the knowledge we have accumulated in our own field as satisfactory and do not wish to explore others' issues. It also suggests that disciplinary boundaries are not convenient administrative fictions but almost unbridgeable gaps between piles of knowledge on whose pinnacles the experts sit. Their privileged vistas encourage tenacious oversight of curricular turf and necessitate distant treatment of the uninitiated. However, it is important to recognize that the organization of our knowledge is a by-product of inquiry, not the thing itself.

Crowds. Finally, even our enrollment practices communicate the wrong things to students. Introductory courses quite typically have double or triple the numbers that other undergraduate courses have. It follows that students receive less personal attention in introductory

60

classes. They also have fewer opportunities to try their ideas out publicly in the classroom and less experience in the give-and-take of critical exchange. The very numbers convey the message: Students are there to receive ideas silently and passively.

What Is to Be Done?

The points about introductory courses that I have raised in the preceding section belie our lofty remarks about good minds and liberal education. The structure of introductory courses results from practical compromises all along the line by trustees, administrators, and faculty. It is no doubt impossible to locate precisely where the bulk of the responsibility for these compromises ultimately lies. Consequently, there is no obvious reason to anticipate any substantial relief from the practical pressures. However, we have not explored other possible responses to these constraints. In the real world of limited resources, compromises are inevitable. The question is whether we have made the best ones. In the space that remains, I suggest some alternatives to the situation just outlined.

Small Crowds. Ideally, no course should have huge enrollments. If some courses must, then they should be in the upper division. If students have had the chance to mature intellectually through intimate and dramatic inquiry in their introductory and lower-division courses, they will have developed the powers necessary to proceed independently in the more crowded advanced classes. By that time we can hope they will have learned a good deal about how to learn on their own. This modification would eliminate the need for holding introductory classes in lecture halls, it would require such courses to receive a much larger share of faculty time, and it would require the students in them to receive a larger share of faculty attention. Although this alternative would probably limit a department's ability to offer upper-division courses, it would ensure that the upper-division courses had hearty enrollments.

Writing. If we restrict the enrollments in introductory courses to reasonable numbers, then grading essays will not consume half of the semester. Students must write. It is through that process that we (and they) learn whether they can simply regurgitate material or whether they have digested it, that is, whether it has become part of them, subject to their control. The only possible compromise when facing huge enrollments is to assign only one or two essays during the entire semester. Few steps can more thoroughly undermine undergraduates' confidence, unless their best grade is disproportionately weighted in the calculation of their final mark.

Unseating Experts. All faculty members should teach introductory courses. They would have to, if departments acted on my first recommendation. Doing so is an excellent way to reacquaint ourselves with our intellectual beginnings. From the construction of the syllabus to the way in which we conduct the class, the teaching of introductory courses demands constant reassessment of our most cherished intellectual and pedagogical prejudices. The mere exposure would decrease the distance between the most senior faculty and not only their students but their junior colleagues as well. Likewise, team-teaching arrangements, especially in introductory courses that cross disciplinary lines, force us, as representatives of our respective disciplines, to face the scrutiny of colleagues from other fields in the presence of students. Such interchanges enhance the learning experience for all concerned. In short, they keep us honest.

Conversation. If classes are not too large, genuine exchange is possible, even in lecture halls. In almost every class, there are at least a few students who are naturally inclined to speak up. It does not take extensive prompting to get people to talk in most situations. Why should classrooms be the exception? Participation should probably be an explicit factor in the evaluation of students' performance, since it almost always is an implicit factor. Eventually, the criticisms of fellow students deter thoughtless comments offered merely for the sake of appearances. Students prove much more willing to contribute if they understand from the beginning that their comments matter not only to the success of the class but to its direction as well. The general strategy enlists the insights and enthusiasm of the best students in encouraging others to try their hand. Learning is exciting, and excitement is contagious. It is so contagious that the conversations will extend beyond the class hour. The more *that* happens, the less distinct the boundary between education and the real world becomes. Learning becomes increasingly central to living.

Conclusion

Whether these simple ideas will promote greater emphasis on the process of inquiry in introductory courses or not, we must somehow revive that emphasis. We must focus strategies in introductory courses on how to compensate most effectively for the practical constraints that we all face, instead of on how to accommodate to them. Otherwise, our task will swiftly become one of merely doling out the facts.

All that is at stake is the development and maintenance of good minds, theirs and ours respectively. The facts age quickly in a rapidly changing world. By contrast, experience at inquiry perfects tools necessary to contribute intellectually and to adjust personally. Even in the best of times, events are mostly beyond our control. The cultivation of exemplary minds is our only justifiable hope in the face of the resulting uncertainty.

References

Eiseley, L. *The Star Thrower.* New York: Harcourt Brace Jovanovich, 1978.

Hutchins, R. M. *The Great Conversation.* Chicago: Encyclopedia Britannica, 1952.

Kuhn, T. *The Structure of Scientific Revolutions.* (2nd ed.) Chicago: University of Chicago Press, 1970.

McCauley, R. "The Business of the University." *Liberal Education,* 1982, *68* (1), 27-34.

McCloskey, M. "Intuitive Physics." *Scientific American,* 1983, *248* (4), 122-130.

Popper, K. *Objective Knowledge.* London: Oxford University Press, 1972.

Rorty, R. *Consequences of Pragmatism.* Minneapolis: University of Minnesota Press, 1982.

Thomas, L. "Debating the Unknowable." *The Atlantic,* 1981, *248* (1), 49-52.

Robert N. McCauley is assistant professor of philosophy at Emory University, Atlanta, Georgia. His major areas of research interest are liberal education, epistemology, philosophy of science, and philosophy of psychology.

PART 2.

New Directions for
Introductory Courses

The introductory science course for nonmajors can prepare students to make informed decisions about the significant biological events in their lives.

A Model Introductory Course for the Life Sciences

Elof Axel Carlson

I was an undergraduate at New York University from 1949 to 1953. I majored in biology and minored in history, an option that was unusual but encouraged by my advisers. The biology that I learned was descriptive. The introductory course consisted of one semester of zoology and one semester of botany. The course was team-taught, with some six faculty members providing the lectures in a large auditorium. The laboratory topics did not seem to be related to the lectures. The rest of my undergraduate major followed a traditional path shared by premedical students and those, like myself, who were determined to become scholars. I took comparative anatomy, genetics, embryology, histology, physiology, and laboratory courses in genetics and histological techniques. There was not much room for elective courses in biology, because the minor, the foreign language requirement, and the breadth requirements were all extensive. I was unaware of the revolution in molecular genetics taking place, and as a would-be geneticist my background for graduate school was classical.

The pace of scholarship was slower in the 1950s than it is today. I did not learn about the Watson–Crick double helix model of DNA until 1954. Many years later, when I wrote a biography of H. J. Muller,

K. I. Spear (Ed.). *Rejuvenating Introductory Courses.* New Directions for Teaching and Learning, no. 20. San Francisco: Jossey-Bass, December 1984.

the teacher who first presented that model to me in his class on muta-
tion and the gene, I learned that he, too, did not know of the model for
some six months after it came out. He was on sabbatical leave in Hawaii
and the university did not subscribe to *Nature*. There were no Xerox
machines then, and Muller's research associate at Indiana University
had to have the pages photographed and then to send the bulky photo-
copies to Hawaii. By 1958, when I received my Ph.D., the revolution
was well under way, and I was learning the vocabulary and ideas of
biochemists and microbiologists. Nevertheless, we graduate students
were told that we should be prepared to teach introductory zoology or
biology and our specialty field when we became instructors or assistant
professors in our first academic position. In 1958, it was still acceptable
to go directly from the Ph.D. to one's first college or university, the post-
doctoral fellowship having just begun to develop as a result of the federal
monies made available after Sputnik.

In the 1970s, the pattern of zoology or botany for the introductory course yielded to a one-year biology course. Description was played
down, and principles were stressed. The new course approach was
accompanied by a shift from separate departments of zoology, botany,
and microbiology to single departments of biology. As molecular biologists joined these departments in the 1970s and the departments swelled
in size, they began to split again, not into their original taxonomic king-
doms but into foci of excellence: molecular biology, cellular biology,
ecology and evolution, and, more recently, neurobiology. The struggle
to be a focus of excellence was often short-lived. Ecology rose in the
1970s and collapsed in the 1980s, as the field hitched its wagon to the
nation's political moods. Behavior biology had a brief spurt of social sig-
nificance before its controversial biological determinism was swallowed
up by the cellular and molecular approaches of neurobiology. The foci
are far from established, and considerable jockeying will continue in
years to come as the life sciences evolve. The pace today, as it has been
since the 1960s, is fast and heady, with new insights and observations
leading to startling realizations about the differences among simple
(prokaryotic) and complex (eukaryotic) organization of genes and their
role in development, metabolism, and evolution.

The Function of an Introductory Biology Course

As a seasoned teacher, I have participated in introductory
courses both for biology majors and for nonscience majors. I have
taught undergraduate specialty courses in genetics, mutagenesis, and
other refined areas of my discipline. I have also been a member of the

committees that designed introductory courses. At a more elevated but less effective level, I was a member of the university's teaching policy committee and even chaired it, each role equally lacking distinction in effecting major reform of the curriculum. I have also had an opportunity through Danforth Foundation and Lilly Endowment workshops on the liberal arts to discuss the teaching of biology with faculty from many colleges and universities.

The biology course for majors today, at least at the larger universities and liberal arts colleges, is intended for the professional development of students. It tries to be an overview of the life sciences today, but that is an impossible task, because the bulk of what goes into the course did not exist when I was an undergraduate, and to accommodate the new fields compromises had to be made between faculty who wanted to preserve whole-organism or descriptive biology and faculty who wanted to inject new life into the field. Both faculties share common interests — students must learn a technical vocabulary, grasp some major principles, and appreciate experimental laboratory approaches. Both faculties also share an erroneous belief that the course is addressed to future biologists. In most institutions it is addressed — often to the disappointment of the faculty who teach it — to premedical and predental students.

The entire department takes a concern in the introductory course for the majors, and the committee that designs it often includes faculty who will not teach the course but who want to assure that their discipline is not shortchanged when the syllabus is finally agreed on. As a result, the course often includes more fields, principles, and descriptive topics than can be taught effectively. The lectures often adopt steamroller tactics, with the lecturer more intent on covering the topics allotted by the syllabus than on determining how well the students receive them. The majors course, I believe, is designed to suit the faculty's perception of what biology is or should be; it is not designed with the student in mind. If it were, committees would discuss the motivation needed for reaching premedical students, the ways in which lower-division students learn, and the objectives of liberal arts courses in a university.

Quite a different tradition exists for the course for nonscience majors. Here, no committee designs the course. Unlike the team-taught majors course, the non-science majors course is usually taught by one person. The course is often classified as a service course, a phrase that suggests the military draft. It is often assigned, by default, to a tenured but unproductive faculty member. Neither the department nor its head seems to care if the course is presented in an uneven or idiosyncratic way. While the majors course is remarkably uniform across the country and reflects committee consensus about what biology is, the non–science majors courses vary in mission and content.

There are watered-down majors courses that attempt to cover what the biology majors learn, but detail is stripped to a minimum, and difficult topics are sometimes omitted. As in the case of the course for the majors, no serious thought about the meaning of liberal arts education enters the design process. While premedical students feel restless about the unrelatedness of life as portrayed in the majors course but continue in their major with the hope that other coursework will somehow get them into medical school, the nonscience majors are often permanently soured on the life sciences as a deadening experience.

Another popular approach for the science breadth requirement is the specific-topic approach. Here, the instructor may provide a course on human sexuality, human survival, or global ecological concerns. The built-in interest of these courses rests on their aspirations to understand or modify political action, but their theme is often sharply focused, and what the biology students learn may be limited to a small fraction of the principles and topics that biology majors experience in their introductory course. The specific-topic approach does fit liberal arts attempts to relate disciplines and stimulate discussion, but sometimes these courses are designed instead to meet the needs of allied health professions. Such courses as human biology (emphasizing how the body works) or anatomy and physiology (often for future nurses) provide fact-saturated topics for students who, like their premedical counterparts, have a clear idea of what they want to learn. These courses are appreciated unless they are poorly taught, although their value for the university's liberal arts goals may be minimal.

Courses that attempt to reach nonscience majors by combining the liberal arts objectives of a breadth requirement with substantial exposure to the life sciences are rare and often reflect the personal interests or biases of the instructor. Such idiosyncratic courses do exist, but unlike other service courses provided by the department, they lack a common core of subject matter or approach. It is difficult to find a text for such a course, and it is equally difficult to teach it with makeshift collections of notes, paperbacks, or readings.

A Successful Model of a Non–Science Majors Biology Course

Since 1968, when I joined the faculty at SUNY Stony Brook, I have taught a non–science majors course in biology. It is a one-year course, but I have on occasion adapted it to a single semester. Most of the students are lower-division students who have not declared a major or who intend to major in the social sciences or humanities. I wanted the course to provide the biology that students need to know in order to participate in decisions involving life sciences and their own lives. I assumed that students would be curious about the biological aspects of the human condition and that they would want to use their knowledge to clarify or form their values on personal, national, and international issues. I wanted them to learn how to engage in informed debate and discussion in a democracy. I based my course on the belief that tomorrow's decision makers on the role of life sciences in society are more likely to be nonscience majors than they are to be biology majors. I wanted to address the future teachers, school board members, journalists, business executives, lawyers, activists, and politicians whose only exposure to the life sciences would be a Biology 101–102 course.

That the human condition has a biological component I did not doubt. I had read vital statistics in almanacs and in the records of the U.S. Census. I had also read enough books in the history of medicine to know that the human condition changes each generation. Today, the biology that we face is quite different from the biology of those who lived before this century. We no longer take infectious diseases and high infant mortality rates for granted, as Third World nations still do. Instead, we face a life cycle in which some 8 percent of marriages are permanently sterile, one in five women experiences a spontaneous abortion, and about 5 percent of babies are born with a genetic or developmental defect. Less obvious to us is the tendency for some 20 percent of us to die in our adult years before reaching old age. All these episodes in our passage through life involve biological processes that we can understand. With understanding comes intervention for treatment and prevention. With intervention comes the conflict of personal and public values, of individual ethics and religious morality, of family desires and social legislation.

As the class learns the cellular mechanisms that lead to birth defects, to cell death, and to abnormal embryonic development, I relate the processes of cell division, gamete formation, and Mendelian principles to agents that disrupt them, life-styles that invite damage to genes and chromosomes, and the wealth of applications to which basic science leads. What was once history or sociology or anthropology becomes part of the liberal arts integration through the biology of the human condition. Students learn that these lectures lead them to their newspapers, television evening news, and their own family stresses. It forces them to confront controversies and to consider options that they might prefer to ignore.

How does a course that relates biology to human experience deal with controversy? In the large classes that I teach, which have between 400 and 600 students, how does one approach a spectrum of values that ranges from permissive liberalism to authoritarian conservatism? How does one address a class that contains Jews, Catholics, and Protestants when discussing elective abortion, prenatal diagnosis, artificial insemination, eugenics, and racism?

Since abortion is clearly divisive in our society, I will use it as an example. I point out to the class that most abortions today are done for social reasons. Some people would not terminate a pregnancy for economic or personal reasons, but they would for medical reasons. Other people would not consider abortion as an option under any conditions, including rape and incest. Most people would terminate a pregnancy that was ectopic (for example, in the oviduct), because its continued development could kill the mother, and the fetus would have virtually no chance of developing fully even if the mother survived. I ask the class why people make so many different responses and what their role is in a pluralistic society that has many religious viewpoints and philosophic differences. I point out that we live with numerous apparent contradictions and that we try to rationalize these into a consistent policy. We may believe it is an evil to abort an embryo or fetus under any condition, yet may also believe in capital punishment or the right to fight a just war. We may also belive that abortion is a woman's personal option, that capital punishment is an evil, and that war of any kind is abhorrent. A simple principle of preservation of all human life rarely exists in our society, and it contains too many strains and exceptions to prevail under all social conditions or emergencies. I point out that it is my responsibility to present the biology underlying controversies, options, and responses, but it is their responsibility as students to incorporate the knowledge that they master into their personal values when they become parents or attempt to shape or alter social policy. Finally, I emphasize that, while I respect the values that many of them have, I as a citizen can differ in my values and that in our society we have to learn to live with diversity and conflict.

In the course, I stress the cell and the gene in the first semester and development, molecular biology, and evolution in the second semester. These five principles are, I believe, the basis of modern biology and give students a view of life that extends from the nucleotides of our genes to the complexities of organisms and populations. It also adds the dimension of time, extends our history to its distant origins, and projects us into an indefinite future for which each generation has some responsibility.

No course is intrinsically good by design. Students attend lectures not only to learn the subject matter but to be intellectually excited by the instructor. An effort must be made, especially in large introductory courses, to engage the students. The skilled teacher, like a solist in a concert hall, has mastery of the subject matter and skills in delivery that make the lectures effective. But, good teaching does not necessarily convey the concern for values, the interrelatedness of knowledge, or the applications possible from new principles and technologies.

Should Majors Encounter a
Biology of the Human Condition?

The curriculum now experienced by most biology majors includes the one-year biology survey and courses in genetics, embryology, cell biology, ecology or evolution, invertebrate or vertebrate zoology, and molecular biology. Biochemistry, which used to be a graduate course, is frequently taken by biology majors in their senior year. Botany is usually omitted or selected as an option by a minority of biology majors. Larger universities may offer more options, including courses in the history of biology or bioethics, but these are often absent from biology departments, and when they are present they are often cross-listed from other departments. It is not uncommon for the biology major to believe that science deals with facts, that it seeks new truths through experiments, and that it is neutral to social values. Indeed, many of those who taught and attended graduate school in my generation believed firmly in the objectivity of science and tried to protect the field by refusing to be involved in public decisions on the use of science.

However, since the atomic bombing of Hiroshima and Nagasaki, many scientists have shifted toward an involvement with society. The *Bulletin of Atomic Scientists* is a forum for such scientists. General professional journals, such as *Science,* permit an exchange of views through letters, editorials, and submitted essays. While scientists thus discuss and debate with their fellow scientists, they seem reluctant to express their views in the classroom. Scientists fear the charge of propagandizing in their courses, since they may not feel sufficiently well informed to express their views on controversies and social policy. They may also feel that it is not the job of biology courses to supply a forum for debating public policy. The danger of such avoidance is that it teaches students that science is neutral and that it is not their responsibility as citizens or employees to question the uses or misuses of their skills. It can lead to the moral neutrality of those who designed gas chambers in Nazi Germany, who allowed black syphilitics in veterans hospitals to serve as untreated controls, or who discharged chemical wastes into rivers without worrying about their long-term effects.

I do not believe that a course in ethics or philosophy is sufficient to compensate for the absence of concern for values in the biology major's curriculum. The introductory course can establish in the biology major's mind at the outset that scientists do not work in a social vacuum. They are responsible for the use and misuse of new knowledge. If that theme is valid for all undergraduates, it is valid for the science majors as well. Just as the course for nonscience majors introduces that biology needed to explore individual and collective decision making and the controversies that it provokes, so, too, can the majors course. The majors course can both deal with the human condition and take a comparative approach that points out the similarities and differences between our biology and that of plants, animals, and microbial systems. While such a course could explore fewer controversies and topics involving the human condition, students would learn that the same principles affect our values as humans in complex ways.

Since most biology majors will have additional course work in molecular, cellular, organismic, and population biology, the downplaying of descriptive biology or broad surveys of animal and plant form and function and life cycles will only delay these topics, not eliminate them from the major's curriculum.

Problems of Curriculum Reform

It requires effort to establish any innovation, whether for a nonmajors or a majors introductory course. In this section, I will mention a few difficulties that I encountered and the strategies that I used to overcome them. How does one teach a large class of several hundred students without an adequate staff of teaching assistants, without clerical help, without a budget, without a text suitable for the course, without the support (or even interest) of one's colleagues, and *with* the need to maintain one's own scholarly productivity?

For the first two years in which I taught Biology 101-102, I was disappointed that only five graduate students had been assigned to staff the fifteen to twenty sections for discussion and laboratory activities. Moreover, the teaching assistants were uneven in ability. Some could barely speak English, one had been told by her major adviser to neglect her teaching, and several looked on their assignment as an insult — they were not even teaching assistants for a majors course. I realized, of course, that every course had legitimate claims for the most enthusiastic or gifted teaching assistants and that I had to look elsewhere for a solution. Thus, I created an upper-division course, a practicum in teaching for undergraduates. I prepared an application form, interviewed applicants and selected a number (about twenty) that made it possible to limit discussion sections to twenty students. I dropped the laboratory as unworkable and too costly. To prevent both the undergraduate teaching assistants and my colleagues from feeling that I was exploiting the teaching assistants, I had them attend a weekly workshop in college teaching. We discussed effective lecture design and presentation, and I made each teaching assistant present a fifteen-minute minilecture to the other teaching assistants and me. We criticized voice projection, eye contact, blackboard use, organization, voice quality, intrusive phrases (*uhs, ers, okays,* and *you knows*), mannerisms, pace of delivery, and level reached.

These seminars were valuable for the student assistants, who also learned how to grade essay questions, how to lead a discussion group, how to tutor (for example, I assigned two or three F students to each teaching assistant and instructed the teaching assistant to sit with the F students individually in lecture and compare lecture notes afterward). I carefully documented how the course would benefit students, how I had arranged a way to prevent conflicts of interest when assistants graded the essay parts of examinations, and how the quality of instruction by undergraduates was better than what the graduate students could provide.

To prevent undergraduate favoritism or bias in grading essays, I alphebetized the examinations and counted off equal numbers of names for each grading group. Students in any one grading group were not graded again by the same teaching assistant. I curved all the returned packets and classified the teaching assistants as hard, fair, or easy. On the second examination, assistants who had been evaluated as hard graders graded the tests of students who had had an easy grader on the first examination. When I returned the examinations, I provided the class with a copy of the grading key used by the teaching assistants. I asked those who felt they had been graded unfairly to justify the questions on which they felt they should be regraded. This forced them to learn the material in dispute, and it gave me a chance to evaluate the grading, because I knew which grading group each request belonged to when I alphabetized the regrade requests. When a teaching assistant erred, I called the person in and went over the papers with him or her in order to improve the grading habits. These didactic approaches and the checks and balances that I developed assured the course committee, which was nervous about instituting an undergraduate teaching assistant program, that I would administer it fairly with the intent of teaching the student assistants a lot about academic life.

I solved many of the other problems by lobbying the university over a period of several years for a course coordinator. I pointed out that in very large courses the unusual becomes the expected and can be time-consuming. Every year, I have students who are sight- or hearing-impaired, otherwise disabled, terminally ill, facing court trial, injured or temporarily ill, or psychologically troubled. These students take time and require special examinations, changes of discussion section, tutoring, and other services. There are also demands for missed notes, a means for distributing graded examinations and homework, and accurate record keeping, which is difficult with a large class. The course coordinator, now five years in this job, handles a majors course of 900 to 1,000 students and my course of 400 to 500 students. The coordinator makes it easier to get handouts typed and run off, examinations prepared, discussion sections switched, and clerical work accomplished. It took eight years to get the position, but the time that it has released for scholarly activity and additional teaching is substantial.

To compensate for a suitable text I supplemented a commercial text with copies of my lecture notes, which are carefully outlined on one side of eight- by five-inch cards. Four cards can be photocopied onto one letter-size page. The master copy is electronically cut, and mimeograph stencils are used to run off the notes for each week, which are distributed by the teaching assistants to students who elect to purchase the notes at cost. The cost is based on the paper, ink, stencils, maintenance, and hours of student labor needed to make about seventy-five pages of notes per semester. I consulted with the university attorney to make sure that the practice did not violate state tax laws or university policy. It is important for the notes to be readable but not complete. They should teach students how a good outline can be used to prepare a lecture, they should be useful for review, but they should not be especially detailed, because students will otherwise not take their own notes.

I eventually wrote my own text for the course, but I had to try several publishers before I found one willing to consider a text for what the editor called an idiosyncratic course. The editor was helpful in making the book marketable, but making it marketable involved compromises on my part: I had to drop some chapters and add chapters on topics that I did not cover. Also, I had to drop my working title, *The Human Condition: A Genetic Approach,* in favor of the rather straightforward title, *Human Genetics.* Nineteen-sixties titles were out, the editor explained. Besides, he added, a publisher can always sell a book at a level lower than its title but not at a level higher.

Many of my colleagues do not welcome sales representatives from book companies. I always do. I share information on my courses with them and try to learn from them how biology is changing in colleges and universities. The resulting exchanges are often as valuable as those at a national convention. Such conversations can also impress on the instructor the realities that a reformer is likely to face. Texts, especially for established courses, change slowly. Publishers cannot take risks on radical departures in course design unless the departures are backed by a national body (as they were after Sputnik) or suggested by discontent tapped by sales representatives.

Finally, what does the instructor do who takes on the large introductory course at the larger university or college that emphasizes scholarly research as a continuous activity of faculty? It is wise for an administration to limit such courses to tenured faculty. The scholars who teach them have to choose their research interests wisely. I have used my sabbaticals to learn new fields or to write books. I treasure my summers for scholarly work. Unfortunately, granting agencies do not support such part-time scholarship. The quality of undergraduate teaching could be substantially improved if there were summer research rewards or fully paid sabbaticals that provided the scholar-teacher with an opportunity to be productive as a scholar for precisely those limited times. It is easy to justify the value of having outstanding teachers teach large introductory classes. They attract majors to the department, they generate full-time equivalency figures for the department, they influence students' career goals, they generate respect for the field, and they stimulate other departments to introduce comparable courses or to improve the quality of their introductory courses. In the long run, they generate respect for the institution among alumni, they help the university to attract good students, and they enrich the democratic and scholarly traditions of the nation. Support for such summer or sabbatical research also supports the scholar-teacher ideal among those who dedicate themselves to excellence in teaching.

Interested readers can write to me for an outline of the Biology 101–102 course as it now exists. It differs somewhat from the text that I wrote for the course in that the text includes a chapter on blood groups that I do not present in the course and in that my lectures present more cell biology and more controversies than the chapters do.

The advantage of relating the human condition to the cell, gene, development, molecular biology, and evolution as I do in this course, is the flexibility that it provides to the instructor. Controversies change, new technologies emerge, values are challenged in new ways every year. This allows the course to shift its emphasis on topics, to introduce new topics, and to drop less interesting ones while maintaining the focus on the five basic concepts.

Elof Axel Carlson is distinguished teaching professor in the Department of Biochemistry at State University of New York at Stony Brook.

What is so important about psychology that it
should be part of every student's general education?
is a question that leads to redesign of an introductory
course.

Reconstructing
Introductory Psychology

David G. Winter

Introductory social science courses are often orphans in the liberal arts
curriculum. It was not always so. In the halcyon days of general education after World War II, we are told, students were introduced to political science and economic theory through the fabric of history and philosophy. They learned psychology in the broader context of sociology
and anthropology. However, the rise of departmental autonomy and professionalism eroded this interdisciplinary synthesis. The introductory
course became a narrowly defined introduction to the undergraduate
major program. Perhaps unconsciously, many social science faculty
even thought of the introductory course as the first step toward an advanced degree and a career in the relevant discipline. Ironically, the
very popularity of the social sciences and their perceived career relevance exacerbated these trends. Students flocked to social science courses
to prepare for helping careers or for law school. As enrollments flour-
ished, social science departments felt little need to attract more students by offering the imaginative, broad-based introductory courses in
the liberal arts tradition that other, less popular departments developed.

All these general trends are especially true of psychology. Just
when student concerns were leading to increased psychology course
enrollments in the 1960s, the breakdown of earlier interdisciplinary

K. I. Spear (Ed.). *Rejuvenating Introductory Courses.* New Directions for Teaching
and Learning, no. 20. San Francisco: Jossey-Bass, December 1984.

perspectives (such as the culture and personality approach of the previous thirty years) cut the field off from its broader intellectual context. New research paradigms and advances in statistical techniques further reinforced psychology's rather self-satisfied isolation within the liberal arts curriculum. As a result, the evolution toward premajor and preprofessional introductory courses probably went even further in psychology than it did in other social science disciplines.

Disciplinary Versus Liberal Arts Perspectives

What is wrong with narrowly defined introductory courses? After all, they are supposed to introduce students to a discipline's methods, theories, and points of view. Early exposure to a field's frontier areas of scholarship should excite and challenge students. It is important for them to have a realistic picture of a discipline. With these aims there can be no quarrel; they are the goals of any good course. The problems of a narrow preprofessional introductory course lie elsewhere. What are they?

First, such courses tend to focus on intellectual issues — concepts, controversies, problems, methods — as they are defined at rarified levels of advanced scholarship, not in relation to broad dimensions of human knowledge and human affairs. In an introductory psychology course, for example, we might push students to master details about neural pathways implicated in the aggressive behavior of rats or the latest laboratory studies of social perception and attribution, because these are active topics currently at the frontiers of psychological research. Do such topics have a place in the introductory course? Perhaps they do, but perhaps they do not. A far more important question for the introductory course is the context or framework in which these particular research facts are embedded: What are the differences between biological, psychological, social-cultural, and other levels of explanation? How is research different from other modes of knowing, and what are its strengths and weaknesses? What are the advantages, problems, and dangers of translating a real-life phenomenon into a laboratory experimental paradigm amenable to systematic manipulation and study? At what point do particular experimental paradigms gather such momentum that further variations are pursued purely for their own sake, well beyond any conceivable relevance to the original problem? For the advanced researcher, these are important questions, but they have long since been considered and resolved. However, for introductory students, they are still lively and open intellectual issues, closely bound up with the rest of their studies and saturated with themes of personal identity and social development. Approaching such issues directly and explicitly, linking introductory psychology to the broad intellectual tradition of the liberal arts, is an obvious way to enhance students' interest, motivation, and learning and thereby their overall development. Yet, these links do not come easily to instructors oriented to the discipline and the profession in their narrow sense. Nor are textbooks stressing the relevance of psychology to students' lives likely to be of much use. Replete with trite pictures, vacuous cartoons, and wide margins, many of these texts address only the most superficial student concerns (for example, school achievement or shyness).

Second, introductory psychology courses intended as an introduction to the profession usually train students in professional technical skills and habits of work. A term paper assignment, for example, might ask students to locate and review several journal articles — perhaps on a narrowly focused research topic or perhaps on a broad theme drawn from everyday life, such as smoking, intelligence testing, or the treatment of emotionally disturbed children. These assignments have dubious pedagogic value for the introductory student. Reading and criticizing the literature on any psychological topic is a skill acquired slowly and with some difficulty. Individual journal articles are highly specific, fragmented, and uneven in quality. What makes a particular article important or even worth reading and what makes a particular journal first-rate are not readily apparent to introductory students. Most journal articles are embedded in a theoretical framework or experimental paradigm that is not explicitly articulated. *Psychological Abstracts,* exhaustive though not evaluative, offers little help. As a result, many introductory students are likely to become quite lost. Library facilities will certainly be severely taxed. Even with sufficient journals and adequate guidance, however, such assignments are far more appropriate for an advanced course or a graduate seminar. Methodology is an important part of scholarly training in any field, but when it is introduced for its own sake in an introductory course it contributes little to the general education of students who never take another course in the field.

A good introductory course, then, is not simply a total survey of the field or an overview of current topics and problems. While it may serve to introduce prospective majors and future professionals to the field, it must also contribute to the general education of all students. Simply put, a good introductory course in any field answers an elementary question: What about this field is so important that it should be a part of the common education of all students, no matter what their college major or ultimate career? Only faculty who are committed to the liberal arts ideal as much as they are to their own discipline can give adequate answers to this question; yet even faculty commitment is not enough. There are some concrete questions that are more difficult to answer: What are the effects of liberal arts education? These effects should presumably be among the main goals of introductory courses. Which of these effects is a particular field in the best position to realize? How can an introductory course be designed to bring them about with the greatest effectiveness and efficiency? What kinds of readings and assignments will work best?

I cannot answer these questions, because there are no simple answers. For some readers, the questions may recall the self-searching of the competence-based education programs of the 1970s. If they do, it does not mean that the competence-based approach gives quick and easy answers. We still need to specify which competencies or outcomes are important, and our knowledge of how to achieve the kinds of broad outcomes or competencies associated with liberal arts education is rudimentary and unsystematic. Thus, the rest of this chapter is a highly personal account of how I recently designed and taught an introductory psychology course. With two colleagues, I had just completed an intensive research study of the effects of liberal arts education (Winter and others, 1981). For the following term, I decided to teach introductory psychology again. While the field had undoubtedly changed in the ten years since I had last taught the introductory course, I was not sure that simply catching up on journals and research review articles was the best way to prepare. How could I apply what we had learned from research on liberal education to the design of the introductory course? Was our research of any practical use to my teaching?

The Effects of Liberal Education

We had shown that liberal education has several important and distinctive effects on students. At the cognitive level, it promotes analytic thinking — the ability to form and articulate complex concepts that order and arrange confusing impressions into usable information. It increases intellectual flexibility and consistency — the ability to deal in rational and sophisticated ways with conflicting arguments on both sides of a controversial issue. Liberal education also makes students integrated and instrumental in their emotional or psychological functioning. It increases maturity of adaptation to the environment, self-definition (an instrumental style of decision making under stress), and disciplined desires for power and leadership. Finally, it increases the realism and differentiation of students' self-knowledge.

How do these changes come about? Different aspects of college experience and institutional structure affect growth in different student characteristics. For example, extracurricular activities, dormitory involvement, sports, control of student conduct, and institutional prestige, among other factors, all seem to have distinctive effects. For designing an introductory psychology course, I was naturally interested in student characteristics that courses and other curricular modifications could change. As one might expect, we had found that the academic aspects of liberal education had their greatest effects on students' cognitive development: "Courses and course programs that present students with both complexity and confusion, on the one hand, and discipline and integration, on the other, will enhance the growth of critical thinking [analytical ability and concept formation]" (Winter and others, 1981, p. 141). That became the starting point for my course planning. So far as diversity and complexity go, psychology is an ideal field, ranging as it does from the transmission of electrical impulses within the nerve cell through the intricacies of psychoanalytic theory to the dramatic and vivid explosions of crowd behavior. Covering even only some proportion of these topics in a single semester can confuse most students. To prevent the introductory psychology course from becoming a vast idea bazaar that overwhelms students and to realize the gains in analytic thinking some kind of integration is needed. The major challenge in developing an introductory psychology course, then, is to work out the best concepts — the broadest, most accessible, and most useful ideas — that psychology can contribute to the liberal arts tradition. These concepts can then become a framework for integrating the diverse material of the course.

Themes to Integrate Diversity

What are the best, the most important ideas that psychology has to teach to all students? For me, the first and most important answer was that psychology offers a vision of human nature — a model (to use a word congenial to my tough-minded colleagues) of the psychological human. What is it to be human? To this age-old question, psychology gives some answers. To be sure, they are not so poetic as the magnificent words of the eighth Psalm: "What is man, that thou art mindful of him? . . . For thou hast made him a little lower than the angels, and hast crowned him with glory and honor." Yet, psychology does offer distinctive concepts and contributions to our ideas about human nature — motives and goals, internal personal organization and the use of information about the external world, individual development and functioning in a social context, and finally the ways in which all these component structures and processes can break down. This image of the psychological human stands in sharp contrast to images offered by other academic disciplines: for example, the economic human or rational actor so familiar to economic theory, political analysis, and (more recently) deterence theory and strategy (for example, Schelling, 1960) or the theological human images that underlie a good deal of the moral history, literature, and ideological rhetoric of the west.

Elements of the Psychological Human

The notion of the psychological human became the overall integrating theme of my introductory psychology course. I began the semester not with the structure of the nervous system but rather with Freud, psychoanalysis, and alternative conceptions of personality. Before taking a psychology course, many students think that this is what the entire field is about, so their interest is aroused from the outset. In terms of the overall integrating theme, this first part of the course emphasizes individual differences (that is, personality) and unconscious motives as alternatives to the idea of men and women as uniform rational actors. For this purpose, the details of particular personality theories and variables are less important than two general points: first, that different people can have different goals and motives; second, that a good deal of personal functioning can be affected and even transformed by the influence of unconscious goals and processes.

Having established that the normal human information-processing functions of perception and memory are subject to disturbance and distortion, the course then turns to the study of these cognitive processes. From the transduction of stimulus energy from the external world to neural energy at our sense receptors through entry into long-term memory, the emphasis is always on the broad, integrating theme: Humans get information about the external world, but limitations of capacity make this a process of creative construction, not of faithful representation. We are able to organize certain features of the environment intelligently, not to remember large quantities of information perfectly. This conclusion has enormous implications for the study of human functioning, and it leads naturally to a focus on the development of intelligence (centered on Piagetian theory) and to a discussion of learning (a field in which so many battles that now seem fruitless were fought between 1930 and 1960).

Since human action, including even perception and learning, always takes place in a social context, the next part of the course explores the social dimensions of human nature. We are what we are by virtue of the influence of others around us—past, present, future, and imagined. Extraordinary obedience, altruism, panic, and prejudice are all vivid illustrations of this social aspect of the psychological human. While no simple explanation can do justice to humanity's social nature, it can be explored from biological, personality, dramaturgical, and social-structural points of view. Here, Milgram's (1975) experiments on obedience to authority provide a good illustration of the transformation of individual behavior in social situations. Milgram's work is also useful for discussing the advantages and dangers of studying human behavior by manipulating variables in a laboratory experimental paradigm, a focus of the course to which I will return. From this perspective, stereotyping, prejudice, and discrimination are a kind of pathology of humanity's social nature acting upon its information-gathering processes.

The course concludes with a brief survey of psychopathology. In line with the broad integrating principle of the course, the major forms of disturbed functioning are conceived of as breakdowns or diminished functioning of the aspects of human nature already discussed: Neuroses are presented as conflicts or disturbances in motives and personality forces; schizophrenia as seemingly abnormal information processing, and paranoia and depression as disturbances of power and affiliation, the two major dimensions of human social behavior. While generally true, these connections are intended more for ease and coherence of exposition than for complete representation of the complex field of causes of psychopathology.

Course Mechanics

These psychological contributions to our image of human nature are the first major integrating theme of the course. Within the material presented in readings and lectures, all sorts of comparisons and contrasts—among personality, cognition, social psychology, and abnormal functioning—can be made in order to increase the integration of such a diverse array of material. Explicit compare-and-contrast essay questions can be given on exams. A modified form of comparison, which is easier for teaching assistants to grade, can also be constructed by asking for the usual identifications and then for a comparison of each of two major concepts, which are parallel but drawn from different parts of the course, for example, *prototype* (cognition) and *stereotype* (social psychology) or *medical model of illness* (abnormal) and *social role interpretation of illness* (social psychology).

More extensive demands for integration can be made in a term paper. Here, I have developed a rather different assignment. In many introductory courses, students are asked to do library research on a particular single topic or to apply one or more aspects of the course to explain some real-world phenomenon, as discussed at the beginning of this chapter. Because I believe that the most important pedagogical goal of an introductory course is to foster disciplined integration of diversity, I developed a term paper assignment that explicitly asks for such integration. Specifically, I asked students to pick some major concept from the first part of the course (personality theory) and discuss how this concept (or the behaviors that it covers) would be explained or accounted for by concepts from some later part of the course (information processing, learning, or cognitive development). For example, how would the Freudian notion of repression be explained in terms of recent theory and research on memory and forgetting? In effect, then, students are asked to compare and contrast concepts that cover the same phenomena from different levels or approaches.

The first time, this assignment was not particularly popular. Some students wanted to write a more traditional paper explaining some real-world phenomenon of interest to them. I was firm about the overall structure of the assignment, explaining how comparing and contrasting abstract concepts was related to my goals for the course and for liberal education as a whole. I did, however, encourage such students to rework their interest in the direction of the assignment's structure. Instead of explaining a real-world phenomenon with one set of concepts, they could use two sets of concepts, drawn from different parts of the course, and then compare and contrast their explanations. In other words, one way of comparing abstract concepts is by examining their success in ordering concrete phenomena. The result, I argued, would probably be twofold: a sophisticated understanding of both sets of concepts and a good explanation of the real-world phenomenon.

Many students have difficulty understanding the assignment or getting started. In subsequent years, I explicitly encouraged students — especially students in their first year of college — to write their paper in terms of some particular behavioral example. In fact, over time I am moving toward providing a few suggested standard examples for students who have trouble understanding the assignment at first. In making the assignment, I also explain how to select concepts at about the same level of generality for comparison. One concept should not be much broader or much narrower than the other. I give an example from history: What is the appropriate comparison to the American role in Vietnam? Something like the Battle of Bunker Hill is too narrow, while the history of the British empire is too broad. Probably the British role in the American Revolution is about right as a comparison. (The Battle of Bunker Hill could, I suggest, be compared to the 1968 Tet offensive, and the entire history of the British empire could be compared to the entire history of the French or Dutch empires.) I emphasize that the paper centers on concepts, not on research. To encourage conciseness as well as precision, I limit this paper to five double-spaced typewritten pages.

While I am not completely happy with the details of this assignment, and while I am trying to make it clearer and more accessible to students, I remain convinced that a term paper of this type is more valuable than a traditional library paper for the educational goals that I set for the introductory psychology course. By asking students to compare abstract concepts, I am trying to promote their ability to develop and use abstract concepts. By asking for resolution of conflicting theories and levels of explanation, I am trying to develop students' intellectual flexibility in handling controversial issues.

Appreciating Research

What is the most important idea that introductory psychology can contribute to the general education of all students? My other answer is *an understanding of the nature, uses, and dangers of research.* We live in a society based on scientific research. Whether as citizens, consumers, executives, or legislators, our students will be bombarded by claims (usually on behalf of the particular project or policy) that research shows. In fact, the results of research are always ambiguous, for alternative explanations can always be advanced to account for the results. Any particular relationship could always be affected by some further, unstudied factor, and any particular difference could always be contaminated by some uncontrolled variable. Research can only be an intelligent guide to policy when the principles and limits of research are understood. Are we as citizens, then, to be at the mercy of the experts who do understand? Obviously, a liberal education cannot train students to become experts in all fields, but it can and must, I believe, equip students to understand the research process in general terms. For this purpose, psychology is uniquely valuable, because a good deal of its important research is still accessible to introductory students. In physics, for example, certain astronomical observations are said to constitute a test of part of Einstein's theories. No doubt they are, but the theoretical background and the particular techniques employed are probably well beyond many college students, especially those who do not take introductory physics.

In contrast, many significant psychological research studies can, with some guidance, be understood by introductory students: for example, studies designed to test aspects of Freudian theory (Rosenzweig, 1943; Silverman, 1976), studies of twins to determine the heritability of intelligence or schizophrenia (Gottesman and Shields, 1972), or laboratory studies of the effect of filmed aggression (Bandura and others, 1963). Students can grasp the nature, problems, and limits of inference in these studies. They can often think of contaminating or additional factors, and they can usually understand how these other factors could be controlled or eliminated. I use these and several other research studies in teaching introductory psychology. I do not intend for students to master the intricate details of each experiment or survey, nor do I want them to survey all the variations on a particular research paradigm in order to determine what for the moment is "true." These are appropriate goals for an upper-level or graduate course. Rather I want students to learn about the research process itself in general terms. I expect them to be able to respond to any new research finding with some understanding of the strengths and weaknesses of the procedures and inferential processes that were used. Given research reports about a new biochemical factor presumed to cause schizophrenia (based on findings of differences between schizophrenics and normals) or given a government survey purporting to discover the causes of excellence in public school systems — to take two topics of perennial journalistic interest — I would expect my students to ask some obvious questions about procedures and inferences. For example, were differences in diet, medication, and activity levels between schizophrenics and normals taken into account? Were ability and social class differences among students in different school systems considered?

I believe that research plays too important a part in our society for its interpretation to be left to researchers and other experts. If liberal education is to liberate students, to free their minds and hearts from the tyranny of new authorities, then it must replace students' blind acceptance with understanding. This is no less true for modern science than it was for medieval theology. Our society is inescapably technological; whether it is to be a technocracy or a democracy depends on the success of liberal education in creating such understanding in citizens as well as in leaders. Because of the accessibility of psychological research, I believe that psychology can make a strategically important contribution to liberal education. Hence the care with which I select and present research in the introductory course.

Introductory Psychology in Perspective

Teaching introductory psychology again after ten years, I designed the course less as a preprofessional introduction or initiation to the field than as an essential component of liberal education. Like all faculty, I have been guided partly by conviction and partly by instinct about what works. I have also drawn on studies of liberal education by myself and my colleagues, both to articulate course goals and to design the syllabus and assignments to meet these goals. So far, I am pleased with the results, and I believe that students find the course stimulating and valuable, if strenuous. Yet, I feel that the course is still very much in the process of development. What I have described here is a process of rethinking introductory psychology, not the definitive introductory course.

Yet, how different is this introductory course after all? I use one of the best standard introductory texts and two supplementary primary sources. The lectures and exams cover material that is probably common to many introductory courses. In fact, I also believe that an introductory course designed along these lines is a good preparation for the potential undergraduate major and a good introduction to a psychology career as well as a valuable liberal arts experience. After all, the issues and questions raised from a liberal arts perspective should be part of the education of all specialized professionals who want to know how their specialty fits into the larger intellectual and social context.

I think it is a question of overarching educational framework rather than of particular details. The approach, the contents, and the assignments of this course are what they are because I am trying to present psychology's fullest and best contribution to liberal education in the introductory course, not because I am trying to cover a field. Many times, the difference can be one of emphasis, interpretation, or elaboration. Often, it may seem to be one of nuance. However, committed as I am to the liberal arts ideal, I think that such differences are immensely important.

References

Bandura, A., Ross, D., and Ross, S. A. "Imitation of Film-Mediated Aggressive Models." *Journal of Abnormal and Social Psychology*, 1963, *66*, 3–11.

Gottesman, I. I., and Shields, J. *Schizophrenia and Genetics: A Twin Study Vantage Point.* New York: Academic Press, 1972.

Milgram, S. *Obedience to Authority.* New York: Harper, 1975.

Rosenzweig, S. "An Experimental Study of 'Repression' with Special Reference to Need-Persistive and Ego-Defensive Reactions to Frustration." *Journal of Experimental Psychology*, 1943, *32*, 64–74.

88

Schelling, T. C. *The Strategy of Conflict.* Cambridge, Mass.: Harvard University Press, 1960.

Silverman, L. H. "Psychoanalytic Theory: The Reports of My Death Are Greatly Exaggerated." *American Psychologist,* 1976, *31,* 621–637.

Winter, D. G., McClelland, D. C., and Stewart, A. J. *A New Case for the Liberal Arts: Assessing Institutional Goals and Student Development.* San Francisco: Jossey-Bass, 1981.

David G. Winter is professor of psychology at Wesleyan University, Middletown, Connecticut. A senior author of a recent research study of the effects of liberal arts education, he has developed innovative measures of educational outcomes.

When the introductory philosophy course evokes cognitive dissonance over philosophical problems in which students are already interested, it can help to develop students' skills in reasoning and assessing arguments.

Confronting Students' Beliefs and Values in Introductory Philosophy

William N. Whisner

According to Bertrand Russell, philosophy begins in wonder and ends in heresy. In the introductory philosophy class, the wonder can turn into tedium, irrelevance, and boredom. One of the central goals of introductory philosophy is to create an atmosphere that stimulates students to think critically about philosophical writings and problems. I will focus on this goal because it is important for the introductory course and because the strategies designed to stimulate critical thought can be generalized across disciplines. In order to stimulate critical thought, it is necessary to overcome the dogmatic tendency, that is, the tendency to refuse to seek out evidence and arguments that threaten the truth or probable truth of one's beliefs. A number of strategies can be used to strengthen the student's desire to engage in critical thought, that is, the student's desire to examine sincerely all the available evidence and all the arguments that tend to support or disconfirm their beliefs.

In this chapter, I will concentrate on two of the most important. Finally, I will argue that these strategies are crucial in promoting critical understanding in the various disciplines of a liberal education program.

K. I. Spear (Ed.). *Rejuvenating Introductory Courses.* New Directions for Teaching and Learning, no. 20. San Francisco: Jossey-Bass, December 1984.

Psychologizing the Course Through Cognitive Dissonance

One finds the seeds for the development of these teaching strategies in the writings of the pragmatists C. S. Peirce and John Dewey and in the psychological writings of Leon Festinger, and the seeds have been further developed by the cognitive developmentalists under the influence of Jean Piaget. In this chapter, I will show how Dewey's prescription to psychologize the subject matter and how Festinger's notion that cognitive dissonance can motivate critical thought provide fruitful starting points for powerful strategies to stimulate critical thought.

John Dewey recognized early that persons engage in critical thought if they have an interest in solving a problem that requires critical thinking. Hence, to stimulate problem solving in philosophy, one must begin with problems that the student has an interest in solving. One can psychologize the subject matter in philosophy if one has knowledge of the beliefs, attitudes, feelings, wants, and interests of students as they relate to philosophical problems. Knowledge of student psychology can be used to determine the philosophical problems that have intrinsic appeal to them. One can cultivate students' technical reasoning skills and their concept analysis skills by showing how these skills help to solve the problems in which students are already interested. Dewey held the developmental assumption that students have both actual interests and potential interests. One can stimulate the actualization of potential interests by showing how they enable one to satisfy one's actual interests.

Typically, introductory students are interested in reflecting about the nature of the good life and the good society. They often show less interest in the analysis of such concepts as knowledge, truth, and belief and in the criteria for distinguishing good reasoning from bad. One can psychologize the subject matter by showing how analysis of concepts and arguments is relevant in answering the questions that students actually have: What kind of life is worth living? What kind of society will facilitate realization of the good life?

The behavioral psychologist William Premack has offered an explanation of why it is efficient and effective for learning purposes to relate potential interests to actual interests. He discovered that one can increase the frequency of a low-probability behavior by making it contingent on a high-probability behavior. Using this principle, one can strengthen the student's desire to analyze concepts and arguments rigorously by showing that such analysis provides better answers to the questions they want to ask.

One can psychologize the subject matter in an introductory

philosophy class by choosing philosophical writings and problems that have intrinsic appeal to the students. One can then order the problems and writings to promote the most effective emergence of actual interests from potential interests. Introductory teachers tend to cultivate technical skills in a vacuum without indicating their relevance to actual interests.

The psychologization of subject matter is a necessary, but not a sufficient, condition to optimize critical thought. Thus, one also needs strategies to strengthen the student's desire to discover new problems and to think critically about them. A strategy to achieve this goal finds its roots in the writings of the cognitive dissonance theorists (see *A Theory of Cognitive Dissonance* by Leon Festinger).

Evoking and Resolving Dissonance

The cognitive dissonance theorists have shown empirically that persons who are aware that they hold inconsistent beliefs are motivated to resolve the inconsistency. One can employ a rational or a nonrational method for resolving the dissonance. The effective teacher can describe and model the use of a rational method for resolving inconsistency. Ideally, one wants the student to resolve the inconsistency by examining all the relevant evidence that tends to support or disconfirm each belief. After a rational survey of the relevant available evidence, the student comes to repudiate one or both beliefs on the basis of the evidence. In some cases, the student will adopt one of the beliefs and reject the other, inconsistent belief. In other cases, the student will reject both beliefs because the evidence for each is too weak. The rejection of both beliefs may lead the student to form a new belief that is more reasonable in light of the evidence. The teacher can strengthen the student's desire to engage in rational critical thought by promoting dissonance and its rational resolution. The student will come to realize that the rational resolution of dissonance is more likely to result in true beliefs over the long run. This realization will lead the student to seek dissonance and its rational resolution.

Let us consider the promotion and resolution of dissonance in a specific teaching and learning setting. The student reads J. S. Mill's essay *On Liberty* and comes to believe that laissez faire capitalism promotes the greatest happiness for everyone. The student also believes the evaluative principle that one ought to promote the greatest happiness. After reading Reinhold Niebuhr's development and defense of the Christian ethic, the student comes to believe that promotion of the greatest happiness for everyone is required by another evaluative principle: that one ought to love one's neighbor as one's self. The writings of

Niebuhr and some of the writings of Karl Marx stimulate the student to think that the unconditional economic freedom of laissez faire capitalism results in an unequal distribution of wealth and political power, which is inconsistent with promotion of the greatest happiness for everyone. The student sees that striking inequities in the distribution of economic and political power encourage those with power to forestall or deny the powerless an opportunity to realize happiness. The student becomes aware of the inconsistency between the belief that laissez faire capitalism is the best economic system and the belief that one ought to promote the greatest happiness of everyone. The student's awareness of this inconsistency motivates a critical thought process designed to resolve this inconsistency. The student sees the necessity of giving up one or both beliefs and begins to examine each belief critically. He or she might begin by examining the ways in which laissez faire capitalism could be altered by legislation that promoted competition and the redistribution of wealth. The student will attempt to determine empirically whether such legislative interference in the economy is more likely to promote the general happiness. The student might finally prefer a form of democratic socialism to liberal capitalism.

However, the student might also continue to believe that laissez faire capitalism is the best economic system, because the increased productivity and the income that it generates make the poorest in society better off than they would be under another economic system. The effective teacher will continue the process of promoting dissonance by showing the student how modifications in free market capitalism increase productivity and make the poorest better off than they would be under pure laissez faire capitalism. If the student opts for democratic socialism, the effective teacher will try to challenge the student with liberal capitalist alternatives designed to suggest that everyone is more likely to realize happiness under liberal capitalism than under democratic socialism.

In the original dissonance situation, the student might also try to resolve the dissonance by modifying the belief that one ought to promote the greatest happiness for everyone. The process of resolving the original dissonance is open-ended, since after the resolution of the original dissonance the effective teacher will promote dissonance in the student's new beliefs.

As a promoter of dissonance, the teacher is engaged in an open-ended process. When students resolve their inconsistent beliefs, they have a tendency to maintain the newly formed nondissonant state. Because of this tendency, they are liable to succumb to the dogmatic tendency to refuse to seek evidence that counters the nondissonant belief state. The effective teacher will continue the effort to encourage the formation of a new state of dissonance.

Incompatible Philosophical Views

One can promote dissonance most effectively if one psychologizes the subject matter and orders the writings and problems in a manner that maximizes the dissonance. This can be accomplished by ordering incompatible philosophical views that have an initial intrinsic appeal. The teacher can provide the best defense for each antithetical position and reserve criticism until the student has formed dissonant beliefs and is engaged in the dissonance resolution process. Some teachers of introductory courses have a tendency to criticize the views of a philosopher as he or she presents them. This strategy encourages the student to dismiss the views of the thinker and prevents the formation of the dissonance resolution process. One ultimately wants the student to examine the philosopher's views critically. Thus, it is best to delay the start of the critical process until the student has made the best case for the philosopher.

Juxtapositions of certain writers can be used to provide possible answers to students' actual questions and thereby maximize their dissonance. For example, one can juxtapose Mill's utilitarianism with Kant's deontology; Mill's defense of laissez faire capitalism with Marx's critique of laissez faire capitalism; Skinner's attack on freedom and defense of environmental determinism with Sartre's rejection of determinism and defense of freedom; Mill's defense of freedom and attack on irresponsible state authority with Plato's or Dostoevski's defense of bureaucratic institutional authority and the restriction of human freedom to promote the common good; Skinner's analysis of the nature and causes of aggression with Freud's account of the nature and causes of aggression; Plato's or Kant's analysis of the role of reason in moral and political decision making with the views of Marx, Freud, and Sartre on the limitations placed on reason in this domain by false consciousness, the unconscious, or self-deception.

Dissonance and Technical Philosophical Arguments

It is usually more difficult to provoke dissonance in students when abstract, technical philosophical issues are involved; however, one can always devise a more complex strategy for inducing it. Let us consider one esoteric philosophical issue: How can one know that material objects exist unperceived? Most students find this issue academic, since they have no good reasons for doubting their firm conviction that material objects exist unperceived. In order to stimulate thought about this issue, the teacher must devise a strategy to induce a belief that is inconsistent with their firm commonsense belief that material objects exist unperceived. One can point out that we can provide a "proof" for the independent existence of a material object by perceiving the existence of the object. Since it is logically impossible to perceive an unperceived object, students begin to wonder how one might prove that material objects exist unperceived.

As soon as students are unclear about how to show that objects exist unperceived, they will begin to think hard about how one provides evidence for the truth of the claim that material objects exist unperceived. The students hold the belief that material objects exist unpercived; they also believe that they do not know how to prove or provide evidence for the belief that objects exist unperceived. Then they begin the process of attempting to discover how one proves or provides evidence for what one always thought was a case of certain knowledge.

The ingenious student begins to see that one logically cannot prove that material objects exist unperceived by perceiving them, since the objects would then not be unperceived. The student will also recognize that one does not need perceptual proof of the existence of an object in order to have conclusive evidence that objects exist unperceived. One might have reasons for doubting the existence of some material object that is unperceived; however, it seems absurd to doubt the existence of all unperceived objects. We could not make sense of the objects we perceive if all unperceived objects did not exist. One hopes that cognitive dissonance will lead students to recognize that there are a variety of ways of providing evidence in support of knowledge claims and that it is a mistake to think that the only kind of proof of the existence or nonexistence of an entity is perceptual proof. Thus, while the issue may appear to be academic, one can get students to work on the puzzle by creating dissonance that produces the doubt that motivates them to resolve the inconsistencies.

In most cases, teachers are mistaken if they think they can get students to think critically about abstract technical problems if the students do not form dissonant beliefs in formulating the problem. It is not enough to present students with inconsistent ideas in the abstract. If students do not believe both ideas, they will not be motivated to resolve the dissonance.

One can employ a role-taking strategy to maximize dissonance and diminish the dogmatic tendency. One downplays the ideological nature of the disputes between incompatible views and constructs a competitive role-taking situation in which each student is asked to make the best case for the views of the philosopher with whom he or she disagrees most vehemently. This strategy encourages the student to try hard to understand the writer's views and to gain some appreciation for the thinker's arguments and conclusions. This strategy can promote tolerance and respect for opposing points of view, it can diminish dogmatism, and in many cases it can also promote dissonance.

Finally, I suggest that one can promote and focus critical discussion by giving students focus questions for reflection between class sessions. These questions can be used to encourage students to think about the relevant issues and arguments so that they are prepared to engage in a focused critical discussion at the subsequent class session. In order to foster the formation and resolution of dissonance, one must formulate two different kinds of questions. One set of questions is designed to get students to refute the philosopher's arguments. The other set of questions is designed to get students to refute the philosopher's arguments. Students should analyze and answer the first set of questions before analyzing the second set of questions.

Applications Beyond the Philosophy Course

One can generalize the strategies just outlined for psychologizing the subject matter and maximizing the promotion and rational resolution of cognitive dissonance to other disciplines. These strategies should also minimize the strength of the students' dogmatic tendency in the various domains of inquiry. In all introductory courses, one is concerned about strengthening the disposition to think critically. For example, in history, science, and the social and behavioral sciences, one attempts to cultivate the critical skills needed for testing hypotheses. In these domains, the student has to assess the strength of the evidence that supports the various hypotheses. One can sharpen the students' skills in assessing evidence most effectively by beginning with the hypotheses that the student already has a tendency to believe. The student will be strongly motivated to assess the hypotheses more rigorously if he or she has to choose between two plausible but incompatible hypotheses. The student will be motivated to show why one or both of the hypotheses is not defensible in light of the evidence.

In some cases the student will be encouraged to assess the evidence by designing a controlled, replicable experiment. In natural non-replicable settings, the student can assess the strength of the evidence by drawing analogies with similar settings and by weighing the internal strength of the evidence (as in some historical, clinical, and ethnographic studies). One can strengthen these evidence assessment skills most effectively by showing the relevance of these skills in confirming or disconfirming hypotheses in which the student already has an interest.

The teachers of introductory courses sometimes attempt to teach evidence assessment skills by dealing with abstract issues that have little or no relevance to students' actual beliefs and interests. It is a truism to say that students do not understand why the skill is worth having. One can approach increasingly abstract technical issues in evidence assessment after students find that the evidence assessment process is intrinsically worthwhile. Students initially view the evidence assessment process as a means for determining whether their beliefs are true or false. However, once they begin to exercise and sharpen the skill, they find that the process of evidence assessment is worthwhile in itself.

One of the goals in studying the arts is to cultivate a critical understanding and appreciation of works of art. One begins with works of art that appeal to the student, and one then encourages the student to form judgments about the work that appear to be inconsistent but plausible. For example, a student can form incompatible interpretative judgments about the symbolic meaning of the white whale in *Moby Dick*. He or she can then be encouraged to examine each interpretation by appealing to the qualities of the story that provide evidence relevant to resolution of the dispute. After examining the elements of the art work, the student may reject one or both judgments because they fail to account for all the qualities of the art work.

One may also find that the interpretations only appear to be inconsistent and that the rich ambiguity of the work justifies both interpretations. One may decide that the white whale can represent God or ultimate meaning or ultimate truth and that each symbolic interpretation is compatible with all the incidents and elements of the story and with the description and interpretation of Ahab's self-destructive quest. Most disputes about the proper description, interpretation, and evaluation of works of art are open to some kind of rational debate and resolution. The work of art provides the evidence for resolving the dispute, and the process of description, interpretation, and evaluation is an ongoing self-corrective process. Nevertheless, one can usually show that some descriptions, interpretations, and evaluations cannot be justified because they fail to take particular qualities of the work of art into consideration.

Conclusion

I am not maintaining that the philosophical and psychological writings and problems and the teaching strategies proposed here even begin to exhaust the means for promoting careful critical thought and the desire for continued philosophical growth. Each teacher of introductory courses needs to find the means to which he or she is best suited, given his or her personality, style, and interest, in order to make the course come to life.

In many cases, philosophers of education argue about the defensible goals of education. However, they tend to formulate the issues in terms that render the proposed goals mutually exclusive. Contrary to the views of the combatants in some of these debates, I argue that the goals are complementary. The debate between cognitivists and affectivists presupposes that one must choose one to the exclusion of the other. I maintain that both goals are significant for an introductory course. It seems clear both that cognitive growth is a necessary condition for affective growth and that affective growth is a necessary condition for cognitive growth. Similarly, the debates between the advocates of process and product and between the proponents of methodology and content create a dichotomy when in fact the two poles are complementary.

I have argued that an introductory philosophy course should play a key role in the undergraduate curriculum. Such a course will encourage each student to think about the relations between disciplines and about how education as a whole relates to one's quest for the good life and the good society. Philosophy is significant because philosophical problems arise in all disciplines. One also must develop one's philosophy of education in order to determine what is worth studying and why it is worth studying. Philosophy should develop the critical, creative, and appreciative skills that are especially useful in problem solving.

One also hopes that the strategies used to achieve these goals will enhance the student's appreciation of the cultural history of human beings. In realizing the value of the cooperative quest for truth, the student should come to understand how persons should relate to one another and to the natural world. Philosophy, in the Socratic fashion, should exhibit why the examined life is worth living and why the examined community life is worth living. When Socrates said that philosophy is the art of dying, he implied that a life worth living is a life for which one should be willing to die. By drinking the hemlock, Socrates demonstrated the authentic relationship between philosophy and life.

*William N. Whisner is associate professor of philosophy
at the University of Utah, Salt Lake City.*

Teaching the introductory course is a continuous struggle to
rescue an element of choice from the pressure of circumstances,
but the student's lifelong view of science is in the balance.

Inquiry and Exploration
in Introductory Science

John L. Southin

The large introductory science course offers a challenge to every professor in the department. To many, the challenge lies in how to avoid
having anything to do with it. For the losers of that round, the challenge
is how to teach it in an interesting way in the face of many discouraging
circumstances. For one, the class is likely to contain a significant number of students who have no interest in the subject, whether they are
humanities students who take the course as their science requirement
or premedical students who take it as a distracting obligatory detour on
the road to riches. Hence, except when topics can be related to sex,
drugs, or cancer, the instructor can be assured of attention and interest
from only a minority of the class.

An equally discouraging factor is the subtly disparaging attitude
of colleagues who belittle teaching accomplishments in general and see
no professional advantage in teaching the introductory course. At
McGill University, there is an annual award for distinguished undergraduate teaching, but some departments refuse to recommend any
professor who teaches only introductory courses. Given that teaching
success at any level counts for little when merits are being weighed for
renewal, tenure, or promotion, it is all the more disillusioning to learn

K. I. Spear (Ed.). *Rejuvenating Introductory Courses.* New Directions for Teaching
and Learning, no. 20. San Francisco: Jossey-Bass, December 1984.

that advantage for distinguished teaching is reserved for those who teach handfuls of the most advanced (and presumably the most receptive) students. Most often, teaching is valued only negatively; that is, successes are all but ignored, and failures are routinely singled out as the ostensible reason an instructor is being let go. In this way, a department gains a reputation among students for being properly concerned about teaching quality while at the same time doing what it wants to do anyway, but for reasons less accessible to the sympathies of undergraduates.

Then, there is the matter of course budgets. At most institutions, departmental budgets are closely related to student numbers, and one of the biggest money-makers for the department is the large introductory course. This does not mean, however, that the money is likely to be spent where it is made. Indeed, those who struggle with overwhelming numbers in introductory courses, where teaching assistants are spread thin and laboratory equipment is often malfunctioning and outmoded, are in a real sense sustaining the small, advanced discussion groups that figure prominently in the department's publicity brochures.

Notwithstanding the many reasons for despair, the lecturer in the large introductory course has, by way of compensation, an opportunity to influence the greatest collection of talented students the university has to offer and to shape their thinking for years to come. Not yet numbed by the quantity of factual material to be memorized or disenchanted by uninspired teaching, the beginning students' awakening enthusiasm for the discipline can make every annual retelling of the subject a fresh and exciting account for the professor, too. As long as one can believe that virtue carries its own rewards, teaching the introductory course can be among the most satisfying of all teaching assignments.

Teaching Large Groups

Large class size is not in itself an impediment to learning. Students are far better off sitting in an auditorium with hundreds of their fellows listening to a well-prepared lecturer in command of the subject who communicates the excitement of the discipline than they are in a small group plagued by a rambling bore who communicates nothing but mediocrity. Large audiences can bring out the best in a lecturer because of their responsiveness and the sense of responsibility that they foster. Wasting the time of a few people in our hearing by thinking aloud is an experience common to us all; doing so in front of a handful of students seems hardly different. The temptation to improvise is always present when the class is small. In contrast, a large class is like a polygraph machine with a thousand pens where evasions, inconsistencies, and irrelevancies are revealed starkly and unforgivingly for what they are: the consequences of inadequate preparation.

A large class permits a certain amount of theatricality, which would be merely absurd in a small one. I introduce this subject with misgiving, however, knowing how quickly the ultimate put-down of a good teacher—"Nothing but an entertainer"—can be trotted out by envious colleagues. But it is undeniable that dramatizing oneself and the subject by appropriate gesture, voice inflection, tone, and timing is essential in capturing people's attention and gluing facts in their memories; these devices can be used with small groups only in the most attenuated form. It is not just with a disappointed eye on the receipt box that a professional speaker becomes uncomfortable with a reduced audience; it is more the frustrated feeling (as Jacques Barzun once remarked) of a dynamo being forced to discharge into a nonconductor.

The final objection to the large class that students frequently raise is that large classes prevent them from getting to know the professor. This, of course, is true, if the comment is taken at face value. For example, one of my classes has more than 700 students, and it is indeed impossible for me to get to know them all, even with the best intentions in the world. It is my experience, however, that the expression of this desire is far more common than the desire itself. Nostalgia for the intimate pedagogical relationship that once existed between medieval scholars and pupils and that survived into the modern age as the Oxbridge tutorial system still exerts a powerful influence on our fantasies about education, but interest in participating in such a relationship has all but vanished among North American students. Most students, especially those who choose to start their college career at a large university, prefer an anonymous and distant relationship with their professors. The result is that the few students who want to have a close academic relationship with a professor usually have ample opportunity to do so, even in the largest classes. The initiative rests with the student and properly so.

However, there are some drawbacks to large classes. The one that I feel most keenly is the need to rely on machine-marked examinations or on examinations marked not by the instructor but by teaching assistants. It is not a matter of exam quality, for I believe that machine-scored examinations can test students' ability to think (as well as their ability to memorize or recognize) as effectively as any other type of exam, provided that the instructor is willing to spend almost as much time making up the exam as he or she would have spent grading an essay examination. (I find that it commonly takes between forty and fifty hours to make up the seventy-odd questions on a three-hour final examination.) The real loss to the instructor, however, lies in his or her inability to determine which of the phrases thrown off in the heat of the moment during lectures have the greatest staying power in students' memories. It is a common experience in reading essay examinations to see one's own phrases or even whole sentences repeated time and again almost verbatim. Most often, there is nothing that seems especially compelling about these phrases; they would have escaped attention altogether except for the fact that the reader now sees them repeated by student after student. I used to make note of these occurrences and used the same phrases in lectures the following years. My expectation was that eventually I could construct a whole course that would be impossible to forget by using just the memorable phrases. Alas, I was forced to abandon the effort when my smallest introductory course grew to 300 students.

Course Objectives: Content

Since the introductory course is a gateway to the entire discipline, it is especially important for its objectives to be carefully constructed and then kept conscientiously in mind as the course unfolds. When the course also serves as the science elective for substantial numbers of nonmajors, the balancing of the many conflicting objectives requires considerable agility, since this one discipline now serves as the exemplar for the whole of science.

The objective that comes most readily to mind and the one that seems to govern the majority of introductory courses has to do with coverage: the need to touch as many bases as possible in the time allotted. Cautionary architectural analogies about the untoward fate of structures with weak foundations abound, and in consequence the tendency to overbuild the foundation, that is, to include much more factual material than is necessary or useful, is also common. The impossibility of presenting everything that is known before everything else that is known is rarely appreciated before such courses become so swollen and unmanageable that they collapse from their own weak logical foundations. The purpose of an introductory course is not to cover a subject but to uncover part of it so as to illustrate principles common to the whole. The facts, then, are not ends in themselves but tools with which the disciplines can be further explored. Just as, for example, an examination of Nabokov's *Lolita* that focused merely on the definition of its words would trivialize a masterpiece, so, too, a compulsive enthusiasm for the factual content of the discipline can abort an interest in a subject at its source. This is not to suggest, of course, that the facts are unimportant. Rather, if science is taught mainly as a collection of facts to be identified, catalogued, and memorized, students are left with the ashes but little of the fire that makes science so exciting. Once an interest in a subject has been kindled, the facts will be picked up easily later on. It is the professor's overriding responsibility to spark that initial interest, not simply to demand the retention of facts, which may soon become obsolete anyway.

Teaching Science as Experimentation

What most distinguishes science from other worthy intellectual pursuits is experimentation. Without it, there would be no science, nor should there be any science teaching. At the risk of oversimplifying the thinking that guided the experimenters at the time of their work, I like to teach introductory biology (my own discipline) as a series of problems: For example, what is the nature of the genetic material? How do plants fix carbon? What is the genetic code? In each case, I then analyze about a dozen key experiments that led to our current understanding of these matters. It is obvious that these experiments must be explained and linked by a fair amount of background information, which must be handed to the student holus-bolus, since not every datum can reasonably or usefully be generated from first principles. However, the experiments provide the framework and motivation for learning and understanding this additional information. It is also obvious that we are not examining these experiments with a view to repeating them, for it is principally the logic governing the choice of experimental material, the overall design or strategy of the experiment, and the deductions made from the results that are emphasized. In choosing experiments to examine in detail, I prefer those that are elegant in logical construction and that introduce organisms, tissues, and techniques that have become part of the experimental repertoire of the field. I am less concerned about whether the conclusions have withstood the test of time. What is more important is their influence at the time when the experiments were performed, for it is a commonplace observation in science that many experiments that reported results now seen to be incorrect nevertheless served to advance the discipline. In science, being right and being useful are not synonymous; it is sometimes more useful to be wrong at the right time than it is to be right at the wrong time.

This emphasis on the experimental approach to science has many advantages. First, it is what science is really all about. What better way of revealing the excitement of science is there than by sharing vicariously in both the triumphs and the miscues of actual investigators — looking over their shoulders, as it were, while they fitted together pieces of the puzzle? Scientific facts become demystified; they are no longer disembodied, disconnected, immutable, written in stone, and taken on faith. Instead, they are simply the conclusions drawn from particular experiments which are valid only so long as the assumptions underlying the experiment remain valid. Many will later be proved wrong, and so will the facts that succeed them. Science is one of the most fugacious of man's intellectual activities, yet it is usually taught as being static and unarguable. After most introductory courses, that is the lasting impression that students are left with, except for those few in the class who go on to become scientists themselves.

Our failure to emphasize the tentativeness of science can have far-reaching social consequences. Take, for example, the heated exchanges between creationists and evolutionists, which, harmless and even amusing in themselves, nonetheless hold ominous portents for the teaching of biological and physical science in our schools. Recent revisions in evolutionary theory and the accompanying expressions of perplexity among scientists have been seized on by creationists as if uncertainty and disagreement were inconsistent or incompatible with scientific explanation. The creationists, whose own mythologies are immutable, are clearly misinformed about the nature of science. They reflect the popular view that science must always be either right or wrong. This view ignores that science is successive approximations of the truth. Unfortunately, science teaching is responsible in large part for this misunderstanding. As we celebrate the everexpanding boundaries of science, we must be equally vocal about the concomitant expansion of our ignorance.

Humanizing Science

It is important to give names to the individual investigators, not as something else to be memorized but to make clear that science advances as a consequence of the activities of real people following modes of thought that are fairly generously distributed among mortals. Indeed, after some initial skepticism, many students can begin to see themselves thinking in similar ways; that is, they realize that one does not have to be extremely bright to be a productive scientist. This may seem commonplace enough to those of us who have sat through science faculty meetings and committees, but the popular conception holds otherwise. By hiding the common sense that underlies scientific data and by obliterating the human element from our accounts, we unwittingly do our discipline a disservice by discouraging capable students from giving it a try themselves.

Lectures should be enlivened with anecdotes about the investigators' lives and about the true—as opposed to the reported—reasoning or circumstances that led to their discoveries. The scientific literature, and textbooks even more, distort or conceal the human side of scientific investigation, with the result that it becomes not an adventure carried on by people with feelings, foibles, and failings but a faceless and cheerless grind engaging automatons gifted with incredible logic and foresight. "It is just as well for everyone," wrote Thomas Mann (1965 [1913]), "that people see only the beauty of the finished work and not its origins nor the particular circumstances that gave rise to it, since awareness of the author's inspirations might often confuse and alienate and so detract from its excellence." Perhaps it is true that great works of literature bubble up from murky depths. I do not pretend to know. I do know that few great moments in science would be much tarnished by examination of the origins and particular circumstances that gave rise to them. The effect of such examination is likely to be a realistic appreciation of science and an enhanced understanding of its methods.

Because scientists have been so good at covering their tracks, it is not easy to ferret out useful anecdotes except by contacting one's own circle of scientific colleagues. In the field I teach, molecular biology, Watson's precocious autobiography, *The Double Helix* (1968) and Judson's more far-ranging account, *The Eighth Day of Creation* (1979) are useful sources, as well as full-length biographies and shorter reminiscences, such as *Phage and the Origins of Molecular Biology* (Cairns and others, 1966).

Examinations

Once the instructor has structured the introductory course so that experimentation is at the core and facts have been pushed to the periphery, he or she must ensure that the examinations reflect what the lectures have emphasized. This is the most difficult change to effect, since thought-provoking questions often become long, complex, and prone to defects when cast in machine-scored format. As already mentioned, it can take half an hour or more to construct a question that will test whether a student understands what constitutes experimental evidence or how changing the parameters of an experiment will change its results and conclusions. By contrast, nothing is easier than to make up simple fact-type questions that engage only the student's ability to memorize and recognize.

To reinforce the point that thinking rather than memorizing is required, I used to make myself available during the examination to answer any fact-type questions that students cared to ask. After all, that is what actually happens in the real world when students want to know something, at least until I can teach them to look it up for themselves in the library. But, classes were smaller then, and exams were administered less formally than they are at present.

Lecturing Style

I have learned to be cautious in making suggestions about lecturing style. Lecturing is one of those activities, like driving or sex, that makes us particularly sensitive to criticism. Moreover, an effective delivery is not a matter of a few tricks to be casually acquired but of an art to be painstakingly mastered. The few pointers on lecturing style that conclude this chapter are intended, therefore, primarily for the benefit of others, not the reader.

First, should lectures be written out in their entirety, merely sketched in outline, or delivered off the cuff? As long as the result is the same — seeming spontaneity — it makes little difference. Whatever works best for you is the best rule to follow. Lectures that are read can be soporific, but the reason why they fail to inspire is that few academics appreciate that difference between prose meant to be read and prose meant to be heard. To read as if you were talking, you must write as if you were talking, and before you can do that you must think as if you were talking. All this flies in the face of everything we have learned about scholarly writing. We normally write book prose, not talk prose. In consequence, lectures are written out as if they were meant for publication. The reader can always look back at what he or she failed to grasp the first time or skip on ahead if the sentence begins to drag. A listener's perceptual depth of field is considerably narrower. Indeed, it may be only one or two phrases long. Ideas, then, must be built up in very simple stages. The main points must be made with simple sentences. Even with otherwise inexcusable incomplete sentences. Illiterate and jarring as visual prose, but quite acceptable, effective, and natural when read aloud.

After the text is written, it is scored for delivery. Pauses are marked, and particular words and phrases are singled out for emphasis or inflection. To do this, it is necessary to read the text aloud while working on it, despite the potential for misinterpretation should office walls be thin. After a while, which can last for years, the task of writing for listening becomes easier, and it can often be abandoned altogether. But, as long as any text is to read, it must be written in aural prose, because no amount of vocal histrionics will ever make academic prose intelligible to a listener.

The lecturer's tone communicates more effectively than his or her words. Hence the teacher must seem to be enthusiastic about what is being taught. However, even the lecturer's evident distaste for a particular aspect of the subject can be turned to pedagogical advantage. Here, the hidden message is, I find this dull, and so might you, but because it is necessary to know this in order to understand the truly interesting material to follow, I learned it despite its tedium. Let's all give it a try. Professors are, after all, human, and continuous effervescence is as suspect at the podium as it is anywhere else. But, when the lecturer's ennui is evident for a substantial part of the course, students can hardly be blamed for failing to become motivated. Finally, one should never say that students will find a particular topic difficult. Nothing is surer to become a self-fulfilling prophecy.

For problems concerning teaching technique proper, the most useful diagnostic mechanism is the video camera. Just as many of us were once startled and dismayed when we first heard a recording of our voice a videotape taken unobtrusively during a few of our lectures can be even more sobering. At McGill University, a campus unit provides this service on request, and a trained diagnostician reviews the tapes with the professor and makes suggestions for improvement of the lecturing technique. The unit can also administer diagnostic and evaluative questionnaires to the class in order to assess particular problems and monitor improvement. An essential feature of this service is its confidentiality. Its services are provided only at the request of the professor, and all its findings are available only to the professor. They are emphatically not available to any college administrator. As one might expect, the professors who were already supremely confident of their lecturing skills were the first to make use of the service. As they discovered unknown faults in their delivery and talked enthusiastically about the salutary effect of the experience on their teaching, others more in need of the service began to request it. Over the years, this unit, which consists only of a part-time video technician and a part-time diagnostician, has led to a significant improvement in lecturing at all levels of teaching at McGill University.

108

Conclusion

What all this argues is that the most experienced teachers need to be placed in charge of the introductory courses. Being the most experienced usually implies being somewhat senior, too, so that the demands placed by handling an introductory course on one's time and talents do not work to one's professional disadvantage. Having made the rounds of conferences, meetings, and similar social-scientific events, one has accumulated a store of anecdotes about discoveries and discoverers that are indispensable in enlivening lectures. Finally, one has had the opportunity to clarify one's perspective on the important differences between thinking and memorizing, between scientific understanding and encyclopedism, between being intellectually demanding and merely piling on more work.

References

Cairns, J., Stent, G. S., and Watson, J. D. (Eds.). *Phage and the Origins of Molecular Biology*. New York: Cold Spring Harbor Laboratory of Quantitative Biology, 1966.
Judson, H. F. *The Eighth Day of Creation*. New York: Simon & Schuster, 1979.
Mann, T. *Death in Venice*. (K. Burke, Trans.) New York: Knopf, 1965 [1913].
Watson, J. D. *The Double Helix*. New York: Atheneum, 1968.

John L. Southin is associate professor of biology at McGill University, Montreal, Quebec, Canada. He has worked extensively with groups involved in improving university teaching at McGill and other universities.

The editor provides additional sources of reference.

Suggestions for Further Reading

Karen I. Spear

As the chapters in this sourcebook suggest, designing good introductory courses requires knowledge of more than the contents of a discipline. Successful courses reflect an understanding of curriculum design, expertise in a range of teaching techniques, sensitivity to issues in student development, and integration of the goals of liberal education into the specific discipline. Although little has been written about introductory courses per se, there is a vast literature in each of these areas. The suggestions for further reading listed here are a selection from recent writing on teaching effectiveness and curriculum design, liberal education, and student development. Thoughtful design of introductory courses requires extrapolation from these areas. To complement these general readings and provide some models of innovative introductory courses, I have also included a list of essays that discuss specific courses.

Teaching Effectiveness and Curriculum Design

Dressel, P., and Marcus, D. *On Teaching and Learning in College: Reemphasizing the Roles of Learners and the Disciplines in Liberal Education.* San Francisco: Jossey-Bass, 1982.
Eble, K. E. *The Aims of College Teaching.* San Francisco: Jossey-Bass, 1982.

K. I. Spear (Ed.). *Rejuvenating Introductory Courses.* New Directions for Teaching and Learning, no. 20. San Francisco: Jossey-Bass, December 1984.

Fuhrmann, B., and Grasha, A. *A Practical Handbook for College Teachers.* Boston: Little, Brown, 1983.

Guide to Effective Teaching: A National Report of Eighty-One Outstanding College Teachers and How They Teach. New York: Change Magazine Press, 1978.

See especially Section 1, The Lecture; Section 5, Case Studies; Section 8, Field Study; and Section 9, Problem Solving.

Lowman, J. *Mastering the Techniques of Teaching.* San Francisco: Jossey-Bass, 1984.

Rudolph, F. *Curriculum: A History of the American Undergraduate Course of Study Since 1936.* San Francisco: Jossey-Bass, 1978.

See especially Chapter 6, "Remedies."

White, A. M. *Interdisciplinary Teaching.* New Directions for Teaching and Learning, no. 8. San Francisco: Jossey-Bass, 1981.

Wilson, R., and others. *College Professors and Their Impact on Students.* New York: Wiley, 1975.

See especially Chapter 16, "Increasing the Effectiveness of Undergraduate Learning and Teaching."

Liberal Education

Bell, D. *The Reforming of General Education.* New York: Columbia University Press, 1966.

Boyer, E., and Kaplan, M. *Educating for Survival.* New York: Change Magazine Press, 1977.

Boyer, E., and Levine, A. *A Quest for Common Learning.* Washington, D.C.: Carnegie Foundation for the Advancement of Teaching, 1981.

Gaff, J. G. *General Education Today: A Critical Analysis of Controversies, Practices, and Reforms.* San Francisco: Jossey-Bass, 1983.

Gamson, Z., and Associates. *Liberating Education.* San Francisco: Jossey-Bass, 1984.

The Great Core Curriculum Debate: Education as a Mirror of Culture. New York: Change Magazine Press, 1979.

Student Development

Astin, A. W. *Four Critical Years: Effects of College on Beliefs, Attitudes, and Knowledge.* San Francisco: Jossey-Bass, 1977.

Chickering, A. W., and Associates. *The Modern American College: Responding to the New Realities of Diverse Students and a Changing Society.* San Francisco: Jossey-Bass, 1981.

See Chapters 1 through 5.

Feldman, K. A., and Newcomb, T. M. *The Impact of College on Students.* San Francisco: Jossey-Bass, 1969.

Knefelkamp, L., Widick, C., and Parker C. A. (Eds.). *Applying New Developmental Findings.* New Directions for Student Services, no. 4. San Francisco: Jossey-Bass, 1978.

Loevinger, J. *Ego Development: Conceptions and Theories.* San Francisco: Jossey-Bass, 1976.

Parker, C., and others. *Encouraging Development in College Students.* Minneapolis: University of Minnesota Press, 1978.

Whiteley, J. M., and Associates. *Character Development in College Students.* Vol. 1. Schenectady, N.Y.: Character Research Press, 1982.

Winter, D., McClelland, D., and Stewart, A. *A New Case for the Liberal Arts: Assessing Institutional Goals and Student Development.* San Francisco: Jossey-Bass, 1981.

Applications in Specific Courses

Carr, J. F. "Fiction and Fact: On Trial." In P. A. Lacey (Ed.), *Revitalizing Teaching Through Faculty Development.* New Directions for Teaching and Learning, no. 15. San Francisco: Jossey-Bass, 1983. On introductory literature.

ERIC. Since 1980, the ERIC system has included a heading on introductory courses. See especially ED 221 093 and ED 223 424 on introductory biology; ED 221 410 on introductory psychology; ED 216 270 on the challenges of the introductory course; and ED 214 830 on introductory world history.

Hill, D. A., and Nelburn, N. "Two Modes of Peer Teaching Introductory College Geography." *Journal of Geography in Higher Education,* 1981, *5* (2), 145–154.

Moreland-Young, C. "Teaching Analytical and Thinking Skills in a Content Course." In P. E. Lacey (Ed.), *Revitalizing Teaching Through Faculty Development.* New Directions for Teaching and Learning, no. 15. San Francisco: Jossey-Bass, 1983.

Moss, G. D., and McMillen, D. "A Strategy for Developing Problem-Solving Skills in Large Undergraduate Classes." *Studies in Higher Education,* 1982, *5* (2), 161–171.

Paternite, C. "Teaching Philosophies and Methods: A Developmental Perspective." In P. E. Lacey (Ed.), *Revitalizing Teaching Through Faculty Development.* New Directions for Teaching and Learning, no. 15. San Francisco: Jossey-Bass, 1983.

Pollack, R. "From Theory to Praxis." In *Columbia College Today.* n.d. On Columbia College's civilization course.

Red, W. E. "Problem Solving and Beginning Engineering Students." *Journal of Engineering Education,* 1980, *71* (2), 167–170.

Robbins, R. R. "Improving Student Reasoning Skills in Science Classes." *Journal of Engineering Education,* 1981, *72* (3), 208–212.

Vaughan, K. "University First-Year General Chemistry by the Keller Plan." *Programmed Learning and Educational Technology,* 1982, *19* (2), 125–134.

Karen I. Spear is associate dean of liberal education and assistant professor of English at the University of Utah, Salt Lake City.

Index

A

Arnold, M., 29, 36
Arons, A. B., 43, 51
Association of American Colleges, 5
Astin, A. W., 110
Ausubel, D., 3-4, 9

B

Bandura, A., 86, 87
Barzun, J., 101
Bell, D., 110
Berman, R., 19-20, 23
Biology: analysis of introductory course in, 65-76; background on, 65-66; controversies in, 70; and curriculum reform, 72-75; function of introductory course in, 66-68; majors in, 71-72; nonmajors course in, 68-71
Booth, W., 3, 7, 9, 13, 16, 23
Boyer, E., 8, 9, 16, 110
Bradford College, core program at, 8
Brown University: collaborative teaching at, 22-23; interdisciplinary study at, 8
Bruner, J., 3, 4, 9

C

Cairns, J., 105, 108
Career education, liberal education versus, 26-27
Carleton College, introductory courses at, 18
Carlson, E. A., 2, 65-76
Carnegie Foundation for the Advancement of Teaching, 2, 9
Carr, E. H., 20, 24
Carr, J. F., 111
Chaucer, G., 15
Chickering, A. W., 110
Climates, for introductory courses, 46-47, 50-51
Cognitive dissonance, in introductory philosophy, 90-95
Copernicus, N., 56

Crick, F., 55, 65
Crossgrove, W., 23
Curriculum: readings on, 109-110; reform of, 72-75

D

Dalton, J., 55
Danforth Foundation, 67
Dewey, J., 3, 90
Dostoevski, F. M., 93
Dressel, P. L., 5-6, 9, 109
Dunham, R. E., 7, 39-52
Dunn, K., 48, 51
Dunn, R., 48, 51

E

Eble, K. E., 109
Education: aims and character of, 25-38; career versus liberal, 26-27; as eating bread, 35-36; end of, 28-30, 53; and ethics, 30-33; means and ends confused in, 27-30; mechanical metaphors influencing, 33-36; mixed messages in, 57-60; process and product in, 53-62; as storage, 34-35, 54-55
Einstein, A., 55, 85
Eiseley, L., 55, 62
Elledge, S., 18
Empiricism: and alleged scientific connection, 55-56; and facts, 53-56
ERIC, 111
Ethics, of professionalism and teaching, 30-33

F

Facts: and empiricism, 53-56; insufficiency of, 56-57; mind and knowledge and, 53-62
Faculty: disinclined, 15; for introductory courses, 45-46, 47-49, 61; as role models, 42, 45; scholarly research by, 75; senior, role of, 13-24, 108
Feldman, K. A. 111

113

Date Due